BOWIEODYSSEY70

By the same author

BOWIE ODYSSEY 70

SIMON GODDARD

OMNIBUS PRESS
London / New York / Paris / Sydney / Copenhagen / Berlin / Madrid / Tokyo

Note to the Reader: The following narrative takes place in 1970 and contains language and prevailing attitudes of the time which some readers may find offensive. The publishers wish to reassure that all such instances are there specifically for reasons of historical social context in order to accurately describe the period concerned.

Copyright © 2020 Omnibus Press
(A Division of the Wise Music Group)

Cover designed by Fabrice Couillerot
Picture research by Simon Goddard

Paperback ISBN 978-1-913172-03-9
Hardback ISBN 978-1-913172-04-6

Typeset by Evolution Design & Digital Ltd (Kent)
Printed in Malta

A catalogue record for this book is available from the British Library.

www.omnibuspress.com

TO SYLVIA
Northern District Primary School, 1970

BOWIECONTENTS70

'Dear Cathy and Claire,

Is there any way at all you can help me? I just don't know my true personality.

I seem to act differently to each person I meet. I give different impressions of myself and I can't stand it any more. I just seem to change all the time. I give the impression to one person that I'm dull, reserved and quiet and yet to another – extrovert, gay, in fact – fantastic! I feel all mixed up . . . will I always be this way?'

ANONYMOUS LETTER TO
JACKIE MAGAZINE, 1970

ONE

'David Bowie has one of those super white
Afghan coats . . .'

THE FIRST SATURDAY of the Seventies and this is news. No, this is *HOT NEWS*. The reason young girls yank each other by Teenform bra straps to be first at the counter slapping down eight pence in exchange for that week's *Mirabelle* and whatever revelations about The Gods its Grapevine column might bring. *Cilla Black is growing her hair! Neil from Amen Corner has found a kitten up a tree!! And David Bowie has an Afghan coat!!! A super white one!!!!*

There he is on the back page too. Down on one knee in front of a bush wearing a lavender suit, tasselled suede bag over one shoulder, both hands limp like something by Michelangelo, hair mousy and scruffy, lips apart, jaw slightly jutting, brows frowning as if he's unsure how to answer whatever question he believes the camera lens is asking. It is not yet the face of someone who knows how to enjoy being a pop star, but there he grimaces, another potential tile in a bedroom mosaic of sanctified dishiness cut and torn from the jamboree of pop weeklies vying for piggybank shakes of copper.

'*HERMIT*.'

Larger, thinner, younger and tuppence cheaper is *Jackie*, screaming in the New Year with 'BIGGER AND BETTER DOLLY BOYS FOR 1970!'

January's 'Man of the Month' is moustached minstrel Peter Sarstedt, *Doctor in the House*'s Barry Evans is 'The Boy British Birds Are All Bats About' and David Bowie is just dolly enough for half a page and a one-word headline. *More Hot News!* Top pop star David Bowie is keenly interested in astrology, hypnotism, the possibility of reincarnation, and he plans to visit Tibet.

'I believe there the monks fully understand the deep subjects which interest me,' says David, deeply. 'They are supposed to shut themselves up in mountain caves for weeks on end and to have just a small meal every three days. It's rumoured some of them live for centuries, and I'd certainly like to find out for myself if this is true.'

Super white coats and monastic fantasies of living to be a 500-year-old caveman on a diet of nothing. The morning after the Sixties the world doesn't know very much about David Bowie, who only became a pop star in its dying gasp.

'*He started learning saxophone, also plays guitar, is clever at art, studied Buddhism and has put on "mime" shows.*'

All true. They just don't say how bad his 'mime' shows were.

'*Age 22. Slim, fair. One eye blue, the other grey. Born Brixton, London, but grew up in Bromley, Kent. He formed one or two groups then started singing and writing his own songs. No fan club but write c/o Philips Records, London.*'

Mostly true. His eyes are both blue but the left looks a greyish brown because each pupil is a different size: his right a punctuation mark, his left an eight ball. The permanent scar of a teenage fight with his best mate over a bird both fancied. And, no, he hasn't a fan club.

'*His father, "a delicate Yorkshireman", recently died. And his brother, who Bowie considers a genius, is in hospital. So most of his tenderness is directed towards his mother who he takes to the* Top of the Pops *studio to cheer her up.*'

Truest of all, but then Penny from *Disc* always is. Fleet Street's high priestess of pop, Penny Valentine has the soundest ears, biggest heart and sincerest pen.

'*David Bowie is an extraordinary human being.*'

She is also in love with him. It is easily done.

DID HE LOVE him too, that delicate Yorkshireman? A question never asked. An answer now lost in a rose bed, the top soil frozen, the ground wet beneath where the black dust that was once the living flesh, muscle and bone of his father had been scattered not five months earlier. There is no plaque, no stone, no cross, nothing to tell the world that Haywood Stenton Jones, known as 'John', was born in Doncaster the year the *Titanic* sank and died in Bromley the year humans first walked on the moon. Nothing of the life he lived, the nightclub he ran and the spotlit dreams that died with it, his active military record, his years of service working for Dr Barnardo's, the two women he married and the two children he bore, both out of wedlock. There is just a patch of earth and plants in a memorial garden near the pergola by the crematorium in Elmers End and the half-orphaned knowledge that the tangible remains of his father, once laid out, embalmed, boxed and incinerated into a billion specks of carbon, have vanished, disintegrated or been washed and blown away. He was there then suddenly not there and from that day forth forever not there. Never to say those things to one another neither were yet ready for. Never to share in whatever happiness, fame, riches, wives, children or sorrows befall the son who one day will himself be ashes, here then suddenly not here, having voyaged the 46 years, five months and five days between upon the desolate sea of a dadless world.

No, there is nothing. Only a rose bed and the bereaved vacuum in a terraced house in Bromley near a railway line and a Victorian pub. The house second from the corner with its upstairs back bedroom where David spent years thinking, plotting, fantasising, wishing, listening, learning, reading, writing, wanking and wondering whether he would ever escape. The same house where his father drew his final breath and where afterwards the telephone rang every evening at 5 o'clock for a week. It was he, David, who picked up the receiver each time and, hearing nothing, interpreted the silence not as a fault on the line but unspoken reassurance from the other side, father to son, that everything was going to be OK. He was careful who he told, and chose not to tell his grieving mother, who still lives in its permanent reminder of widowhood until a buyer can be found and a past severed. And when she does, and when it is, and the house on Plaistow Grove belongs no more to the Jones family, should the phantom 5 o'clock caller ever trouble its telegraph wires again, the ectoplasmic crackles will no more be understood.

★

3

A VOICE CALLING from elsewhere. An unidentified singing object bleeping into the charts in the winter of '69 from the outer edges of its radar screen. A voice not *from* outer space but going there. A voice which in its first syllable of fame is already non-terrestrial, neither on earth nor in heaven. A fame which still rests on one solitary song about the solitariness of space, which as of Big Ben's first chime of 1970 remains the sum total of the public measure of David Bowie.

The single, David's tenth, was released in July '69. It took three months to break the atmosphere of the charts, temporarily hindered by a blanket 'space song' radio ban that over-twitchy moon-shot summer before burning up like a Perseid shower at number 5 the first week of November. With only 60 days left of the Sixties, with television having only just turned colour on all three channels, with the 'Town of Tomorrow' already half-built on the south-east bank of the Thames, with a moon newly scuffed by man-made silicone boots hanging in the winter sky beside stars beckoning ever bolder mechanical efforts to reach them, with the Stanley Kubrick film that inspired the song's title still haunting cinemas like the Ghost of Christmas Yet to Come, David's hit resonated as an elegiac fanfare for humanity's fears of what the Seventies might bring. 'Space Oddity'.

Its tune was sad but familiar. Penny from *Disc* hit the bullseye in her first review. 'Mr Bowie sounds like the Bee Gees on their best record, "New York Mining Disaster".' Which he did. She also compared the backing to 'a cross between The Moody Blues, Beatles and Simon & Garfunkel'. Love is blind but Penny isn't deaf.

'Space Oddity' was a song about space made to *sound* like space. Weightless, because of the strings of the young cellist Paul Buckmaster swooping and diving like the aurora borealis. Futuristic, because of the Stylophone, the small toy-like electronic keyless keyboard first passed on to David by a casual friend, its 'Telstar' buzz a cartoon audio shorthand for ray guns and rocket ships. Lonely, because of the unnerving pathos in David's voice and the childlike Jack-and-Jill simplicity of his lyrics telling the story of a spaceman who fell down and broke his crown. Fame found David Bowie in 1969 the same instant it found the tragedy of Major Tom. It was impossible to say which appealed more to the public. The singer, the song or the all-too-believable story of a lone astronaut bound for the moon whose rocket malfunctions, stranding him beyond the help of Ground Control who can only listen with increasing despair to his fading distress signals. David sang 'Space Oddity' not as a narrator but as its doomed hero, staring helplessly at the pale blue dot shrinking ever smaller through the craft's porthole.

The ballad of the loneliest man in the universe.

THERE IS A MANSION on a hill, shaped like a fat spider with two-storey pavilioned wings jutting out from an imperial Transylvanian body. Purpose-built for the mentally enfeebled not quite a century ago, it has its own coat of arms, this granite lifeboat of the damned. A quartered circle surrounded by the Latin motto *Aversos compono animos* – 'Bringing relief to troubled minds'. Within it, the Cross of St George over the River Thames, a Saxon jewel, butterflies to symbolise psychiatry, the wand of Aesculapius to symbolise medicine, and the Southwark Cross to represent its South London catchment.

Each spider leg contains different wards, segregated male and female, bearing the names of scientists, poets, painters, authors and local gentry: Chaucer, Dickens, Faraday, Turner, Wren and the like. They rarely perform lobotomies any more, but they have, and there is still electroconvulsive therapy and, when needed, straitjackets and padded cells. These days they prefer to sedate with chemical hypnosis – Largactil, Tofranil and Stelazine – and so the nurses, male and female, many black and foreign, are but shepherds of the walking dead.

Each day its thousand or more vacant souls rise for breakfast. Those men allowed to shave themselves must queue up to be lathered by a supervisory nurse in communal bathrooms where the showers are bare brick and the peekaboo toilet doors like horse boxes. They wash like prisoners and shit like animals. They do not have their own clothes but wear whatever they're given from the spoiled tweeds, bleached greys and faded navies that return from the laundry the same unifying hue of dehuman. The cafeteria breakfast is a choice of porridge, prunes, kippers or bacon and eggs. The tea is loose-leaf and, for the nurses' ease, mixed in the urn with milk and sugar, then poured as one with the shade, grain and taste of pissed-on sand. Mid-morning there is more tea and biscuits. Lunch is fruit juice, meat and two veg, pudding and custard. Mid-afternoon there is another round of gritty tea and a slice of cake. At 6 o'clock, more meat and two veg. They eat mechanically except for the ones whose motors have broken, bibbed and dribbling, helpless zombie babies who must be face-scrubbed at the table by starch-aproned mothers of finite patience.

They have daily work, if they're capable, in the laundry, the kitchen or vegetable garden. There is basket weaving, art classes, needlework, Bible quizzes and visiting classical musical recitals. There are televisions in the lounges, occasional film shows in the big hall and a shop that sells cigarettes. There is a pitch-and-putt course, a swimming pool and an enormous Gothic chapel for those seeking yet more numbing sedation other than that already prescribed to antagonise their dopamine receptors. Beyond the walls, all around, is woodland: wildflowers and trees, beeches, crab apples, rowans, hazels, hollies, dogwoods, horse chestnuts, oaks, limes and Norway maples. And a graveyard, no longer in use, where the bones of old incurables rot in whispered warnings. Beware the inescapable clutch of The Cane.

Under a green blanket in a single metal bed surrounded by other occupied single beds, overlooked by sash windows with orange curtains in a ward named after the mystic poet and artist William Blake, lies the man he calls 'brother'. Not a Jones, like David, but a Burns like his mother. Terence Guy Adair. Half-brother Terry. The illegitimate cub of a Frenchman named Wolf who vanished before his bastard was delivered bawling on a bonfire night between the wars.

National service did its best to make the boy a man, taking him overseas under the wing of the Royal Air Force where he took things he shouldn't have and saw things he wished he hadn't. Things which he carried home with him in shaking sobs and waking nightmares. Things that made him see the ground catch fire and the sky crack open, made him hide from the world for days on end in local caves till they found him, labelled him and sent him here to Cane Hill. Where he lies now aged 32, ten years older than the half-brother who considers him a genius. Half the genes. Half of what he is. Half of what he may yet become.

THE BLUE FIAT CAR that was once the father's sits in a stony drive on Southend Road, a suburban highway north of Beckenham Junction station. A giant of red bricks, white fascia and timbered gables raised in the middle of the 19th century, the house at number 42 stands detached and grimly palatial. The architecture is a Quaker mass of pious intentions succumbing to the Gothic grandeur of mid-Victorian industrial wealth. As christened: Haddon Hall.

In the age of steam this would-be Thornfield was once the baronial fortress of a Wandsworth candle magnate who, if not for gas lamps, might have burned his profits in wicks to illuminate its infinite shady nooks, snugs, crannies and hidey-holes. From afar, the west-facing façade looks like a chapel. From up close, the east-facing rear is no less humbling: a veranda with carved columns and balustrades opening out onto a landscaped garden of ornamental tree species rolling all the way to the hedgerow bordering the golf course. Even its woodshed has stained-glass doors. The setting is idyllic yet the structure foreboding. It is a house built for midnight screams and ghostly turns of the screw, an altar ready-made for scenes of demonic incantation as trembled upon the page by the pens of Wheatley or Lovecraft.

Impervious to war, Haddon Hall was almost flattened by the Nazis when a doodlebug exploded only a few feet away. The edifice survived the blast but its guts would soon fall victim to the whim of its former gardener, a Mr Hoy, who inherited the property to fillet into separate apartments as he desired. The largest, Flat 7, consists of the whole ground floor, including its main hallway and grand staircase which splits in two at the rear wall of the house beneath a triple-rowed arcade window inset with stained glass. The stairs either side lead to opposite landings that reconnect at the far wall into a square walkway; once offering access to upstairs rooms, they are now sealed off from the first-floor flats occupied on one side by Mr Adams and his family, the other by Mr Charles. A staircase to nowhere, but a nowhere that remains exclusive to the occupants of Flat 7 for £14 a week.

Downstairs the doors are heavy and oak, the walls newly painted white, the ceilings moulded with a repeating simplistic Quaker pattern, the floors cold to the bare foot, tiled, tongued-and-grooved, every inch bleached and scrubbed to eradicate the territorial scent of the 18 cats not long departed with the previous tenants, two elderly nutty professors. A grand stone fireplace squats opposite the foot of the stairs in the corner of the hallway, its various rooms leading off on either side.

On first entering, immediately to the left lies a tiny kitchen in what was once a cloakroom. Next left, the largest of its three main rooms, for now a living room by day and flophouse by night. Behind it, a small bathroom. Over on the right-hand side, two sizeable bedrooms, both with bay windows: the rear overlooking the veranda and garden; the front facing the main driveway. These rooms and the people who sleep in them will change, as will their various colours, uses and purposes. It is the strange nature of Haddon Hall that it warps the memory of all who visit, whether there for a single night or several months, each witness to a particular moment of metamorphosis, not only of the house but of its main occupant. Dadless son, half-brother of a genius, national pop star.

'Big year for David Bowie.'

Mirabelle's 1970 Pop Prediction. There's every reason it should be: *big* and *super* like his Afghan coat. So long as David comes up with another massive hit. Something unexpected and otherworldly to hotwire the public's heart and lasso their mind the same way 'Space Oddity' did. Something *new*. Something *now*.

Something that sounds like the unknowable but inevitable wild new sound of the Seventies.

TWO

THE SEVEN-DAY NEW YEAR hangover subsided, London 1970 looks no different from London 1969. The same cars, the same clothes, the same booze, the same fags, the same illuminated gods in Piccadilly Circus flickering the same gospels of Cinzano, Skol and Coca-Cola. But then eras never arrive with finger-clicking suddenness on the stroke of midnight.

Soho humps and moans from Tuesday night into Wednesday morning. The same old circus that never left town. The small world of Sammy Lee and the big bad world to every horny hayseed stumbling off at Euston with a wallet stuffed for clipping in the first joint flashing an X. Beaded curtains and Maltese muscle. Bow ties at the door and framed photos in the window. Dry mouths licking lips over girls with slap thicker than Christmas marzipan. Pale crescent tits nothing like the ones in the pictures outside, forbidden to jiggle by the letter of the law. Live, non-stop, no membership required. Sin now, pay later. *Roll up! Roll up! Step inside Sodom and Gomorrah, WC1!*

Or step away. Walk northwards up Wardour Street, past the dulled booming from the Marquee club, past The Ship where a fezless Tommy Cooper dares the world and its fools to interrupt his solitary pint, led by the nose of the New Shanghai to a Victorian lamp post missing its shroud of 19th-century fog standing sentry to a thin pedestrian passage. The kind of alley you'd expect to find Lonely waiting on the corner for Callan, home to more indiscreet fleshpots, a cobblers, a turf accountant and an otherwise unassuming door with a barely noticeable buzzer on the wall. In industrial days past it marked the entrance to a fortress of ink, plate, press and printer's devils, until two years ago when Norman Sheffield, his brother Barry, their shared dreams and ten tons of plasterboard transformed this former engraving works into a modern recording studio. They named it after a British jet airliner, to symbolise the business trio of the two brothers and their third-party investor. Trident.

The first group to make a Top 10 hit here was Manfred Mann with 'My Name Is Jack', about a hippie dosshouse in San Francisco nicknamed 'Garbo's' after a poster of the lonesome goddess displayed in its foyer. Weeks later, The Beatles came, beating a retreat from the sterility of Abbey Road to *na-na-na-na* in the same basement. Blessed with the Midas dust they scattered behind, when the nine-time loser at 45rpm known as David Bowie arrived the following summer with his song about Major Tom, in Trident he found his Ground Control.

The flight director who guided 'Space Oddity' to success is a delicate arranger of decibels called Gus Dudgeon. Songs about space, astronauts and rockets bring out the best in Gus. In 1968 he had a Top 5 hit as co-producer of The Bonzo Dog Doo-Dah Band's 'I'm The Urban Spaceman'. Once he found the right stratosphere for David, 'Space Oddity' did the same. Gus is now trying to work similar Buckmaster-string magic on other singer-songwriters including a mystical Yorkshireman named Michael Chapman and a young pianist from Pinner called Reg, currently making his debut album at Trident under his chosen alias 'Elton John'. It won't be a long, long time before Gus is back in orbit.

But in these, the early hours of the last day of his 23rd year, though David is back in Trident, Gus isn't. Tonight there's a different backside in the chair behind the mixing desk. One that, like David's, also rises and shines every day in Flat 7, 42 Southend Road.

Tony Visconti is a friend and more than a producer. A Brooklyn renaissance man, he can write, play, sing if needed, score and arrange. Tony knows how music works, how the business works and as a 25-year-old ex-heroin addict has a pretty good idea how people work. He has professional enough a pop ear to attempt a flower power ballad with Billy Fury and trippy enough a weird ear to coax the Lewis Carroll bong-pop of

Boeing Duveen and the Beautiful Soup. With his East River confidence, draft-dodging kudos, surfer's teeth and eyes a bit like Mr Spock, Tony is a hit with British hippie chicks. The British groups seem to love him too. Every time Tony speaks, his Italian-American accent is a little puff of glamour to the unwashed hopefuls on the other side of the glass who've been no nearer New York City than the last time they saw Officer Dibble on the telly.

So it was for David when he first met Tony in the Summer of Love, bonding over smoke, sci-fi, Buddhism and mutual transatlantic fascination before either of them mentioned music. Tony had just left the States and an unsuccessful career as half of a beatnik duo with his soon-to-be ex-wife for a one-way ticket to the Oxford Street offices of a new production company run by Moody Blues producer Denny Cordell and David's music publisher, David Platz. David had just released his debut album and was on the hunt for new producers for its follow-up. Tony was talented, eager and American, and while David was only looking for the first two attributes it was the third that sealed it.

Had he wanted to, Tony could have produced 'Space Oddity'. David asked him and like an idiot Tony said no, which is why the job went to Gus. The reason Tony said no was because he thought the song was 'too gimmicky' – in the same breath forgetting his were the fingers on 'Jabberwock' by Boeing Duveen and the Beautiful Soup. But he still produced and played bass guitar on the rest of David's second album, called simply *David Bowie*, the same as his first. And now that they live together Tony won't be so silly as to refuse David again.

That's why he's back at Trident tonight, to try to make amends by producing his own Top 5 smash for him. He'll be playing bass again alongside a new session drummer named Godfrey who usually plays frizzy-haired soul in a band called Gass. And then there's their lead guitarist. An old friend he and David have known for many years who Tony's invited in the hope he'll be their sonic secret weapon. Although there's always the danger this one might backfire.

THE SECRET WEAPON has so far given Tony a brace of Top 20 albums – both bedsit flashes in a pan of mung beans, in one week, out the next, and two minor hit singles in the lower 20s and 30s: 'Debora', about digging and redigging a girl who simultaneously looked like a zebra, a stallion and a sunken galleon, and 'One Inch Rock', which while possibly rude made even less sense. But though fanciful gibberish, there was something beguilingly beautiful about the sound of the songs and the way they were sung, as if conjured into audible vibrations like a sonic genie uncorked from the dried ink prison of an Arthur Rackham illustration.

The music, made by just two people, was the eloping din of an acoustic guitar running away with a set of bongos, encouraged by the added capers of kazoo, Chinese gong, finger cymbals and something called a Pixiephone. It fitted the voice floating above in elfish wisps like soft invocations muttered in prayer to forest gods of dawn and dusk, constantly flinching in startled bleats wild with rutting fever. Such a voice, unaffected by all fear of the ridicule it would attract, was unlike any ever to have risen to the surface of popular music: a strangulated gypsy blues trembling in tandem with the mystical Eastern raggle-taggle beneath. It was maximum pop escapism, rock'n'roll as imagined by Edward Burne-Jones starring Elvis as Lancelot serenading an endless succession of Ladies of Shalott, as conjured by a mad sonic maelstrom pounding Hare Krishna, The Everly Brothers, Bilbo Baggins, William Blake, Eddie Cochran, Edmund Spenser and a five-pack of joss sticks together in the same witch's pestle and mortar. A sound called Tyrannosaurus Rex.

Tony has just finished recording his fourth album with this curious duo who've recently undergone a 50 per cent line-up change with the arrival of a new percussionist whose looks, like his name, are a pulverising knockout. Mickey Finn's undemanding role requires only that he casually flick his palms across a pair of congas and leave the rest of the work to the Jesus sex face resting on his neck like a classical bust on a gallery plinth. The sort of face that makes Brontë sisters write novels about women like themselves being driven to unthinkable extremes of irrational behaviour for the love of such a face: Byronic, buccaneerish, poised with the guarantee of deliciously administered bastardy. And Mickey is only Tyrannosaurus Rex's shadow.

The light of the group, its zooming close-up, its symmetrically perfect pretty visage, its impish smile sparking schoolgirl swoons, its Romany curls and dandy lashes, its trembling gizzard and Narnian mind,

12

its metropolitan mod in meadow hippie's clothing, was Tony's other best friend and the secret weapon he's invited to Trident. A singer not quite nine months younger than David, born the same year in the same city but on different sides of the river. Just as talented and every bit as ambitious, possibly even more so. And just as David wasn't born a Bowie but changed his name from Jones, so Mark Feld decided that the outside world would be more disposed to his genius if they greeted him in the guise of Marc Bolan.

Two of a singular kind, born under opposing rock'n'roll stars – David on the day Elvis Presley breathed his first, Marc on the day James Dean breathed his last – the probabilities of location, age and interest threw them into each other's magnetic fields in the full swing of Sixties Soho, circling one another in clubs and coffee bars, mutual hustlers forever passing on Tin Pan Alley chasing the same elusive dream of singing success. They were mirror images of endless resilience unmitigated by serial failure, both inventing and reinventing their identities in impatient metamorphosis from bluesman to mod to folkie. Both were sponges, differing only in how they squeezed. David, restless, impulsive, precocious, unsure whether to commit to the pop world or the theatre where his strident voice perhaps better belonged thrilling the moneyed classes under spotlight and safety curtain. Marc, bright and cunning, his eye fixed firmly on the distant horizon of rock'n'roll glory, impervious to any ill omens insisting he'd never get there. David was a born observer, concocter, copier, actor and assimilator with a talent and appetite to be anything he chose to be from one day to the next. Whereas Marc had always known, whatever the cut of his hair, trousers or musical jib, that he was put on this earth to be a rock'n'roll star. David learned and did. Marc just was.

The sands of the Sixties had been running out for both. David, a King Bee, a Manish Boy, a Lower Third and a Riot Squadder; Marc, a lone pedlar of hippie gumbo and one of John's Children. Nobody noticed either of them. In psychic sync, each retreated into fantasy, David laughing with gnomes while Marc walked with dinosaurs. The name Tyrannosaurus Rex implied music of weight and ferocity, not the cross-legged mantras maypoling around his latest obsession with *The Lord of the Rings*. He'd explain he chose it to remind people there were once animals stalking this earth so fantastic and beautiful they made fools of people who didn't believe in dragons. Tyrannosaurus Rex played griffin grooves for dragon dudes.

It was Tony who unearthed them in a fuggy basement on Tottenham Court Road, playing to a small but enrapt stench of hairflickers all squatting on floor cushions. Signed by his bosses as a hippie novelty, their first album was made in four days and cost a couple of hundred pounds. Expectations were as low as the title was long – *My People Were Fair And Had Sky In Their Hair . . . But Now They're Content To Wear Stars On Their Brows*. It cheekily cavorted to number 15. Two more Tyrannosaurus Rex albums followed in less than a year, their third, *Unicorn*, charioting to number 12. Not quite 'a pop star', Marc now bopped at the top of the underground.

David was still sinking somewhere below, a Bromley tortoise unable to keep pace with the Hackney hare. The friend in Marc helped his old Tin Pan ally as best as his thin skin would allow. When David started experimenting with his dreaded 'mime' shows, Marc invited him on tour supporting Tyrannosaurus Rex so his graceless flops could be heckled by hundreds. When Tony asked if Marc could sing backing vocals for David in a ramshackle studio choir, he was there gaily wailing, giggling and hamming Temptations on-the-spot spins at the microphone. But that was September 1969. When Marc was an underground somebody and David still a no-man's-land nobody. Then 'Space Oddity' charted. And, fuck, it hurt.

It hurt because David's single went Top 5 and Marc's last hadn't even scraped the Top 40. It hurt because every time Marc heard 'Space Oddity' he heard the sound of the Stylophone like a cruel mechanical cackle reminding him he was the big dope who'd given David the instrument in a freak whim of selflessness. But mostly it hurt because David was now unequivocally a pop star. The cover of *Disc*. Pin-ups in *Jackie*. Breakfast plays on Tony Blackburn. *Top of the Pops*. And Marc wasn't.

Tonight, he still isn't. But here he is in Trident, all five foot five of him in his green ladies' shoes from Chaussures Ravel, in his mind already a superstar, and in her mind too.

Because wherever Marc goes, she goes.

*

SHE WAS HERE too last September, roped into that same ramshackle choir for David. She is Marc's manager, driver, promoter, protector, keeper, carer and soon-to-be wife. He prefers to describe her as a white star, tangled and far, a crawling sensation and astral vibration born to be his unicorn. Her name even sounds like one of his songs. June Child.

Four years older than Marc, June is wise, assertive, opinionated, with a carefree tumble of mousy hair and sultry eyes that can seduce or destroy in a guillotine blink. They are the all-seeing optics of one who has seen and done and wants to do more. Eyes that have batted off Syd Barrett and Eric Clapton before they finally locked on Marc over a bowl of muesli. It only took a couple of spoonfuls to realise they loved each other.

Home was briefly a mattress in the back of a van on Wimbledon Common. Now it's a top-floor flat among the hippie ghettos off Portobello Road, a hubble's bubble from the Dog Shop and a Rizla in the wind from the offices of *Friends* magazine, flanked on all sides by Eastern chanters and West Indians bound by the same loathing of the law. Blenheim Crescent is typically Notting Hill: the landings littered with broken prams, the smell of soul food, the paint peeling off the stairwell leading to their lofty haven. Rugs, cushions and walls painted a rich blue. Books upon books, volume upon volume of Greek myths, English folklore, William Blake, Arthur Machen, Kahlil Gibran, tales of the supernatural and J. R. R. Tolkien. On the mantelpiece an ornamental figure of Pan who Marc calls 'Poon' and often prays favours of. A record deck and the stacked black gold of London, Coral and RCA Victor. Satin scarves and more ladies' shoes and fluffy coats and leather bags. Acoustic and electric guitars, a cheap organ and a reel-to-reel recorder in the spare box room dubbed 'Toadstool Studios', with its black-and-white posters of Eric Clapton and Jimi Hendrix tacked to the walls. And a tower of notebooks from Woolworths with spotted covers costing sixpence, each stuffed with poems, songs and stories in Marc's spiky dyslexic hand.

This is the scene in their little Rivendell W11 as they leave it just after midnight before slipping into the AC Aceca parked outside. June starts the car and turns south onto Ladbroke Grove, heading east towards town: Marc in the passenger seat, his guitar behind them, and a boot rattling violently with thunderous second thoughts about where they're heading.

★

15

AS MARC AND JUNE weave through the post-theatre traffic another unscheduled visitor to Trident makes his way on foot through the furtive glances of Soho. He's spent the evening nearby at the Talk of the Town checking on another of his clients, the American jazz singer and bandleader Billy Eckstine. So it seemed impolite not to drop by on his way home. See how things were going with his boy. Because even though tomorrow he'll be a young man of 23, to Kenneth Pitt, 47, David will always be His Boy.

He's been His Boy for the last three-and-a-half years, ever since David Jones became David Bowie and Ken became the boy's manager, bankroller, fixer, promoter, advocate, educator, uncle, chaperone and gatekeeper. Ken is what polite society blushingly refers to as an unmarried bachelor. Oscar Wilde first editions and a teddy bear called Bobby. Suit, shirt and tie, receding reddish hair, parson's spectacles, lungs that inhale antiquarian bookshops, art galleries and afternoon recitals, buttocks that are rarely happier than when pressing down on stretched velvet in the front-row balcony of the London Palladium. That's Ken.

There is very little Ken hasn't already done for David and even less he still wouldn't. It was Ken who, four years ago, returned from his American travels with the sleeveless acetate of an as-yet-unreleased debut album by a new group called The Velvet Underground, its central blank label signed by their mentor, the artist Andy Warhol, its grooves like a home electronics kit instructing David how to entirely rewire the circuitry of his musical brain. It was Ken who wrote the sleeve note for David's 1967 debut album, likening his observational songcraft to that of 'an articulate eagle', moving so fast that 'everything he did was two years too soon'. It was Ken who personally funded a half-hour film intended as an international show reel for David, which, though never screened, first prompted the writing of 'Space Oddity'. It was Ken who'd wined him and dined him and weaned him and preened him up Shaftesbury Avenue and back again, who'd pricked the Is and slashed the Ts on countless contracts, who'd wrestled extra monies and forwarded loans from his own purse never to be repaid. In return, what David has done for Ken is knowledge to none but Bobby and the other mute furnishings of Ken's Manchester Street flat where David once lodged and frequently returned as either's business or pleasure necessitated. Which made him His Boy.

The boy is nowhere to be seen when Ken first arrives, buzzed in from the alleyway and turning right into the control room, its walls slatted with planks like a Swedish sauna. Tony sits in command of the mixing desk, a stainless-steel monolith of knobs, dials and faders teasing with warp factor thrills snug in a tight teak surround. Ken greets him with a puny smile of barely concealed mistrust. It was Ken, ever the fixer, who first brought Tony into David's life three years ago when scouting for a new producer, a decision he's been regretting in increasingly agitated increments ever since. Ken does not like Tony. Not his good looks, nor easy manner, nor his seen-and-done-it-all New Yorkness, nor his accent honking like Fifth Avenue gridlock, nor his wigged-out vocabulary of 'bread' and 'drag' and 'man'. Least of all, Ken does not like the way Tony encourages that aspect of David which Ken understands least, that which involves long hair, loud speakers, low lighting and all the cuckooland colours of Kensington Market.

The woman sitting behind him looks cut from similar hempen cloth. Ken's never met June but knows her type. Decorative rings, brocade dresses, the sort of vixenish hippie boys like David are in danger of finding attractive. Oh, no. *Has he?* Ken's greenest fears begin to surge when June says something to Tony about Marc. It's the way she says it. Heavy petted. 'Marc.' *Her* boy. Mystery solved.

Ken relaxes. He forces a smile at June. She forces one back. The beauty of King's Road recognises the beast of Savile Row for what he is. Envoy to envoy, their pupils dilate, wary irises flickering.

June strikes first. 'You're David's Mr Ten Per Cent, aren't you?'

Ken fumbles for a comeback. 'I don't work *that* cheaply!'

June smirks, blinks her lids, and another head rolls into her basket.

BELOW THEIR FEET in the 60-foot basement, surrounded by tiles of polished cork, sound screens, carpet, wood and yet more wood, David hears none of it. He sees only Ken's flannel trousers flapping in the strip window, looking in on him from the floor of the control room above. So Ken's here. David softly groans.

It's not that he dislikes Ken. He might even love him as a cat loves the sound of an opening fridge. But it's the cold love of a memory, a photograph of love taken years ago, its warm colours faded after too long in the sunlight. David knows he must change the picture in the frame and replace it with another. He just doesn't know how to tell him. Poor old Ken. *It's not you, it's me.* Even if David knows it's not him, it's Ken. Ken who comes here tonight from the Talk of the Town. Ken who will always be Talk of the Town, never *Top of the Pops* – theatre box for a head, bouquet toss for a heart.

David should go upstairs and speak to him but chooses to skulk below where Marc now itches over a white Stratocaster adorned with an odd-looking enamel teardrop. He signals up to the window. An 'OK'. The tape spins. The sound of David, his Hagstrom 12-string, Tony's bass and the drummer from Gass in his ears, Marc scratches. There is music.

David has chosen two songs to record, hoping one will prove a strong enough follow-up to 'Space Oddity'. Both are love songs: one to a person, one to a city.

The person song is 'The Prettiest Star' – as in the silver screen, not the night sky. It's a sweet melody, the tune bumping and swaying, the words wistful and a little maudlin. But it doesn't sound like a hit.

The city song is 'London Bye Ta-Ta'. It's two years old and shows its '68 vintage in a Cockney *um-diddle-i* second cousin to the pearly jingle of the Small Faces' 'Lazy Sunday'. The words are meant to be about immigrants struggling to find their cog in the great machinery of the metropolis, but it's really about David's own capital identity crisis. The Brixton boy who, aged six, got squeezed out beyond the boundaries to suburban Kent, exiled in a distant galaxy at the end of ten miles of rail track.

'London Bye Ta-Ta' doesn't sound like a hit either. It only sounds like the title theme to a potential TV sitcom starring one of the Likely Lads.

Monday
9.30 London Bye Ta-Ta
Starring Rodney Bewes
Comedy. A young man from the North moves to the Smoke but wonders how long he can survive there.
PRODUCED BY THAMES TELEVISION.

Even if it already exists.

Monday
9.30 Dear Mother … Love Albert
Starring Rodney Bewes
Comedy. A young man from the North moves
to the Smoke but wonders how long he can
survive there.
PRODUCED BY THAMES TELEVISION.

The theme to ITV's *Dear Mother . . . Love Albert* is sung by Bewes, who also wrote the lyrics: it's no better or worse a tune than 'London Bye Ta-Ta'.

These are the two gowns which Marc is expected to embroider with threads of Fender gold. On the 'London' song he merely echoes the main melody, scuffing a wonky wah-wah as he goes. He does the same on the 'Star' song, dot-dashing a simple seagull cry over the blank space between verses. Both are 'Three Blind Mice' to fingers accustomed to high-voltage fugues for dancing dawn damsels. Marc is bored, but so is the rhythm. The drummer from Gass flutters and splutters, wallops and plods, unable to make the 'Ta-Ta' ta-dah or the 'Star' swing. Tonight in Ground Control there'll be no lift-off.

Ken's face is a portrait of defeat for different reasons. He waits just long enough upstairs to finally speak to David, to remind the boy about tomorrow night, his show at the Speakeasy and the men from *Jeremy*. Then, without looking at June or Tony, Mr Ten Per Cent slips away into the chilly black dawn. To home, to Bobby the bear, and the elegant silence of his empty bed.

Marc is ready to go too, but June is not yet finished. She has been listening to him streak what comet tails he can through David's lumpy constellations and her verdict is no different to the one she walked in with over an hour earlier. Why should a slipshod understudy like David expect a leading man like Marc to be his second fiddle? She gathers her things and walks to the door but stops when her face is inches from David's.

'You know you don't deserve him.'

The lashes droop and the blade falls.

'You're not worthy of Marc's playing. He's too good for you.'

June turns and glides into the corridor, a benignly satisfied dimple in her cheek. Behind her Marc dithers, his panicked deep-brown eyes unable to hold contact with anyone else's. He jerks something like a smile, but at what and to whom David has no idea. A shake of black curls, and he's gone.

The gravity in the control room crushes. Tony cannot speak. David cannot see. Dumb and blind among a million sparkling smithereens of ego.

THREE

IN BEDROOMS in Bedfordshire, the biros flow bilious. 'British pop music goes into the Seventies with "Two Little Boys" at the top of the charts. What a portent for the future!' Disbelief spills from the postbag of the *New Musical Express*, who are just as confused as Joan from Henlow as to why the last cymbal splash of the Sixties, as bequeathed to the Seventies as its opening snare roll, should be a music-hall weepie about the American Civil War sung by a 39-year-old Australian painter, singer, wobble-boarder and Stylophonist familiar to millions as the host of his own Saturday night light-entertainment show.

'Two Little Boys' took Rolf Harris to number 1 on 14 December. Despite the best efforts of Elvis Presley, Kenny Rogers, Bobbie Gentry and Glen Campbell, he's still there. It's now sold three-quarters of a million copies. A survey of record shops by *Melody Maker* reveals the culprits to be very young kids and their mums and dads. Teenagers would still much rather buy Tamla, Trojan and the new one by Badfinger.

'I know some people knock "Two Little Boys" and call it schmaltz but I really don't agree,' wobbles Rolf. 'To me, schmaltz would be something with sickening over-emotionalism about a cute little baby or something. This is just a straightforward, unashamedly emotional story about genuine feelings and it fits naturally into a storyline. Name me any other record in the charts and it's almost certainly about some form of human emotion. There's no crime in that.'

The biros keep bleeding and the teenage tills ringing for Tamla. But next week Rolf will still be number 1 and the new decade still in its coma.

THE MEN from *Jeremy* are waiting. They lean against the black marble bar, cradling drinks so reassuringly expensive they daren't sip them at less than ten-minute intervals. The music is conversation-killing loud, the wallpaper garish Indian, the ambience a deliberately dingy scarlet; anyone unaccustomed to its murk might think they've mistakenly stumbled into a photographer's darkroom. Pretty things bump and frug in tight stitching, their buckles, boots and loose necklaces twinkling in the murky rouge like fireflies. It is all the men from *Jeremy* can do to stand there, ogling and seldom sipping, idle referees to a game they're neither young enough nor flash enough to partake in.

Jeremy is a new magazine launched four months ago from an office a few streets away in Fitzrovia. *Jeremy*, in its own words, 'is for people who simply don't care about sex − one way or the other. Who have got their values straight.' *Jeremy* is six shillings' worth of glossy eulogies to Judy Garland, *Midnight Cowboy*, 'ambisextrous' photo spreads and an interview with Bee Gee Barry Gibb (favourite cologne, 'Fraiche by Balenciaga'). For those seeking to wage war on the 'old shibboleths' of less enlightened generations, who wish to know which clubs are a 'boutique assistant's paradise' and who appreciate such pearls of black type as Peter Wyngarde's defensive aside, 'My tailor is a closely guarded secret,' *Jeremy* is six shillings well spent. And though it need not be spelled out, the advertisements in *Time Out* do so with pride: *Jeremy* is 'the only gay magazine'.

The men from *Jeremy* are here in the Speakeasy because David is here to perform on the night of his 23rd birthday. They've been shadowing him for the past six weeks: from a spot in the Save Rave 1969 charity bonanza for invalid children at the London Palladium to his own gig at the South Bank. So far he's told them he's 'a loner', has no desire to be 'a leader' and his principal heroes are a hotchpotch of old vaudevillians and pre-war sweethearts including George Formby and Gracie Fields. All this will be printed along with a review of tonight's performance in next month's special 'Valentine issue' between adverts for Dear Roger trousers and *Jeremy*'s own 'fun underwear': the Peeping Tom, in see-thru stretch lace 'to present your credentials'; the Dolly Boy, in supersmooth brushed nylon 'for super dolly people'; the Royal Flush, made of glitter nylon 'to shine in the dark'; and 12 shillings and sixpence worth of the Package Deal in teez towelling 'for hot summer nites'. Inserting David in *Jeremy* is very much Ken's idea.

David mixes his own songs about spacemen and hangmen with the Belgian squalor of Jacques Brel and the more obscure American wisecracks of Biff Rose and Mason Williams. It's not enough to bedazzle the pretty things of the Speakeasy, their applause polite but scattered. They like what they see more than what they hear, and before the night is through an assailant's hand of unknown sex steals a squeeze of David's loins as he passes through the crowd towards Ken's table. The amused men from *Jeremy* make a note and underline it: David is irresistibly gropable.

THE FREEZE is thawing but Beckenham still shivers. Nothing like as bad as the freeze of '63 but it still claimed five lives this Christmas. Chemists have run out of pill bottles in a losing war against influenza. The ABC has *True Grit* but outside the road remains icy and inside the pipes remain lagged.

On Southend Road, Haddon Hall chatters awake. In different rooms on different mattresses in different corners its different bodies slowly stretch to consciousness.

There is David in David's room, possibly alone.

Next door, there is Tony and his girlfriend Liz in their room overlooking the garden. Tony first fell for Liz during a dope whitey and kept on falling after the dope wore off. Liz is as friendly as she is mysterious. Simply 'Liz'. When it comes to her surname she likes to play Rumpelstiltskin. 'You'll have to guess, but I'll give you a clue. It's a brand of jam.' Robertson's? Golly, no. 'Keep guessing.' She's creative on both sides of the easel, a student and a life model. Liz designed the ornate enamel teardrop that sits above the pickguard on Marc's white Stratocaster. She's yet to meddle with any of David's.

Across the hall, there are the nightly bunkers in the big living room: John, David's drummer, and Roger, their roadie. Sometimes other bodies elsewhere, up the stairs to nowhere on the square landing. Friends staying late, staying over, staying until they find their own place to stay. Occasionals like Nita, a local teenager finishing her A-levels who likes to sing Leonard Cohen and chat about The Beatles and Buddhism. Skylarkers and cloudheads for whom there will always be a pillow to dream on in Haddon Hall.

Roger is an Aussie-Cockney and possesses the best of both vocabularies. 'You fackin' kant!' That's Roger. 'Roger the Lodger'. He came to Haddon Hall part and parcel with John and the white van they'd been using for John's main group, Junior's Eyes, who Tony paired up with David last summer to double as his own band. John would have drummed on 'The Prettiest Star' instead of Godfrey from Gass had he not been in Scotland touring with Junior's Eyes. He only got back the night of the Speakeasy gig where the birthday boy asked a last-minute favour to join him on stage with Tony on bass. The men from *Jeremy*, mesmerised by David's 'luminous elfin face surrounded by an aureole of blond curls', took no notice of either.

John is mostly John but sometimes 'Cambo', to rhyme with rainbow not Rimbaud, short for his surname, Cambridge. He is a Yorkshireman, and a very good one. A right laugh, a proper pint and a solid game of darts. That's John. When David hears Yorkshire he hears the unshakeable trace of his own father's voice. He is fascinated by accents, like an actor listening, deconstructing and mimicking. *'Eee, lad, get thysen tut bulludy barbers!'* But John's is a softer Yorkshire. The flat East, not rugged West. Born and bred in Hull, where they call a spade '*a sped*' and a guitar '*a geetah*'.

If the court of Haddon Hall needed a jester then John is happy to jingle the bells. A bag of water pistols is produced and men turn into boys, hiding and seeking, finding and squirting. David chases Tony behind sofa, up staircase and round garden while in the kitchen John lays ambush with a newly emptied washing-up-liquid bottle. The trap is set and David caught in the full drench of the Cambo water cannon. When the soaking stops and the clothes dry there is always a ball to kick around outside and Instamatic cameras at hand to capture team portraits of Haddon Hall Wanderers: David, smiling mischievously in a stripy jumper, chin out like a victorious team captain, John beside him, arms crossed like Bobby Charlton, surrounded by long hair, skinny jeans and happy faces. Memories preserved like messages in bottles to a less innocent future. Conversations about UFOs and mysterious energies. Windows blowing open and knocks from the spirit world. Late-night records, smoke, singing, games of darts and dirty laughter. This is David's Paradise Found. Even if *he* never actually found it. *She* found it, and Haddon Hall isn't home without her. But she is not here.

She is the other half of David and David the other half of she – neither he nor she complete without the other. They'd barely moved in to Haddon Hall together when she left to return to her family in Cyprus at the end of November. David has written regular love letters care of her parents' house in Xeros, including a Christmas card pleading she come back and be his wife. But, over a week later, she hasn't replied.

David has yet to connect his silent letterbox with stories in the papers about a Christmas backlog – in excess of a million letters are still stranded in sacks in Royal Mail sorting offices. His friend Mike is a postman but David never thinks to ask him. He just sits and frets and writes more letters until in desperation he decides to telephone Xeros long distance. She answers.

By fateful synchronicity she's received his letters and the card with the marriage proposal that morning. Before she can give her answer, David has something he wants her to hear. An acetate of the song he recorded a few nights ago in Trident, the song she inspired him to write and the reason he'd wanted to record it with the hope of serenading her 2,000 miles back to Beckenham. She was his Prettiest Star.

She listens while the acetate spins, David holding the receiver to the speakers so she hears every word about their rising up all the way. When the song is finished he can hear sobs. Happy sobs. Then she says yes. She will be his wife.

Before she hangs up she tells him she'll be catching the next plane to London tomorrow. It is all David wanted to hear.

She is coming home.

SHE IS 20 years old, two and a bit years younger than him, roughly his height, hippie-slim, slender-limbed and flat-chested, shaggy tomboyish brown hair, an open face with a wide, excitable mouth and big, sharp eyes that can obliterate hell in wide open cannons or illuminate heaven in snapped clamshells of laughter. She's been a student of business and economics at Kingston Polytechnic, before that at a Connecticut women's college where she was expelled for lesbianism, before that at a Swiss boarding school where she harboured thwarted ambitions of becoming a ballerina. By birth an American-Cypriot, which carries its own visa issues living in the United Kingdom, this is one of the reasons she's agreed to marry David. He wants her back, and to bring her back to British soil he knows he'll have to marry her, even though he's already told her to her face that he does not *love* her. This is an arrangement she is nevertheless prepared to accept. Because she is the singular force of nature christened Mary Angela Barnett. Formally Angela. Informally Angie. And she loves him.

They've been as one less than a year. Angie met David through her friend Calvin, a fellow American and a fellow bedfellow of David. Calvin was an Oriental renowned for his magnificent apparel, sometimes wearing a reflective silver 'love jewel' in the centre of his forehead, a 'doctor' with a PhD in pharmacology who had chosen to focus his intellect on the more chaotic chemistry of artist and repertoire for the London offices of Mercury Records in Knightsbridge. It was thanks to Calvin that David signed the deal with Mercury resulting in 'Space Oddity'. And it was thanks to David and his shrewd understanding of how success in the record industry often boiled down to a willingness to lie back and think, if not necessarily of England then of being number 1 in its charts, that Calvin had instigated the contract.

Angie's first fleeting fascinated glimpse of David was in the autumn of '68 at an all-nighter in the Roundhouse; singing halfway down the bill as part of a folk trio alongside the woman who would disfigure his emotions to a shape and state beyond repair. There is smitten, there is bewitched, and then there is the calamity of reason when David met Hermione. *Her-mi-on-ee*. The name belonged in a fairy tale and so too the spell she cast. David believed he and Hermione were to be together forever, two handles on the one loving cup of eternal paradise. She could sing, she could dance, she could just about act; she was Baez to his Dylan, Fonteyn to his Nureyev, Bacall to his Bogey. They had the same bone structure, the same spindly arms, the same locked gaze of infantile infatuation, but markedly different blood: hers was gravel driveways and polished silver; his was tarmacked terrace and antimacassars on the back of the settee.

The girl from upstairs and the boy from downstairs spent the best part of six months living together in idyllic sin in a top-floor flat in South Kensington. David was aged 21¾ and would mark this period in a future résumé of his life thus: '21¾ – Fell in love.'

He did, body and soul.

Then Hermione left him for a role in a film about the life of composer Edvard Grieg, shot on location in Scandinavia. His heart went with her and never returned. What she did with it was anyone's guess. Those who knew David well guessed she must have tossed it in the Baltic. The shell-shocked 22-year-old she left behind, picking out the shrapnel one agonised lyric at a time, was a different creature from the one who'd succumbed to her all-consuming enchantment. Now he realised 'Fell in love' had been a near-death experience. David would never make that mistake again.

It was this self-preserving love-proof David who, on Calvin's invite, Angie finally met, dined, danced with and bedded on a Wednesday night in April 1969. They clicked not just physically but intellectually, aspirationally and pansexually. Neither were beholden to the social and religious expectations placed upon their respective genitals, nor at whom the procreative laws of land and heaven decreed they ought to thrust them. Sex was freedom, and in the glorious guerrilla coupling of David and Angie sex had no more devoted a pair of freedom fighters. Theirs would be less a fleshly pact than a spiritual revolution.

Their courtship was acted out in full view of David's new landlady, a hippie journalist and single mother named Mary, the downstairs neighbour of an old school friend who invited him to lodge in the spare room of her garden flat in Beckenham. She introduced him to the wonders of tincture of cannabis and he introduced her to the wonders south of his midriff. Mary was in love with David and remained so even after she woke up one day to find Angie sharing their breakfast table. Broken hearts not being in vogue that season, all three learned to live in harmony at the height of fashion.

For want of space rather than cramping style, Angie rented another love nest for them a few miles away in Blackheath – sharing with some of Mary's friends, the editors of a new hippified listings magazine called *Time Out*. Then, that August, David's father died. He briefly moved back home to Bromley to comfort his mum, inviting Angie with him. To the grieving Mrs Jones David was her angel, but his friend Madam Satan. The tension of Plaistow Grove removed any last doubt that they needed a place of their own and in the estate agents on the bridge by Beckenham Junction station Madam found it. Flat 7, 42 Southend Road.

Home.

DAVID IS THERE waiting to meet Angie at Heathrow Airport. They embrace for the first time that year, that decade. Fiancé and fiancée.

Soon the masonry of Haddon Hall is rattling to her familiar returning fanfare, as unmistakably American as the hum of a Boeing Superfortress over inland Japan. Angie is loud in a world she knows will not listen were she any quieter. Her noise is a hurricane of impatient intent. Each moment a living dress rehearsal for the movie of her life – one day to star Bette Davis, driven by the same battle hymn, riding into the field with sword gleaming and standard flying, ready, willing and able to conquer the world. A reality to be experienced at 24 frames a second, each much too precious to waste on the cutting-room floor.

The lord and lady of Haddon Hall retire to their pastel blue bedchamber to re-anoint. Outside, on the golf course beyond the bottom of the garden, the still winter night is thrashed in coital concord by the violent yelps of mating foxes. Above them, the prettiest of stars, a scattershot infinity of lights pulsing hundreds of years out of the past, posing endless questions to the future. Just hanging there waiting to be wished upon.

FOUR

FINGERTIPS FLUTTER OVER the tops of paper sleeves. Marc is not yet so famous that he can't negotiate the record stores of Tooting and Wimbledon in broad daylight. The greasy-haired assistants behind the counters feign ambivalence though they clearly know who he and his bearded Man Friday are.

John Peel is a disc jockey with his own BBC radio show on Saturday afternoons. Eight years older than Marc, he's been his most loyal advocate on air, in print and behind deck for the last three years. Even without the encouraging fug of pot and incense perfuming John's humour, it is love by any other name. For music, poetry, Scalextric and each other's company. Last year Marc gave John the gift of two hamsters called Dandelion and Biscuit; John set up and named a record company after the first and a publishing company after the second. John has also guested on two Tyrannosaurus Rex albums reading Marc's stories about elves, goldfish gauntlets and mushroom parchment. Whenever together they are Merry to each other's Pippin.

Marc hasn't travelled five miles over the river just so he can listen to John rave about freaky forgotten beats by The Toggery Five in his sleepily restrained ghost of a Scouse accent. Marc's mum and dad, Phyllis and Sid, live here in the same prefab where they dragged him as a reluctant teenage refugee from Stoke Newington, displaced from his north-easterly centre of gravity and the city streets where his dandy suits flushed like winning hands, his face an ace even at 14. A king, however young, never forgets losing his crown. Whatever Marc is and will yet become carries the scars of his years of exile in Summerstown, SW17. The little prince lost in space.

Marc's best spoil of the day is a five-year-old single by The Sorrows, 'Take A Heart'. John tells him there's a better, brassier version by The Boys Blue, but, as he sometimes is, John is wrong. Marc remembers 'Take A Heart' like the imprint of a kiss from his debutante autumn of '65, just turned 18 and shooting for the moon with his first record, 'The Wizard', 100 seconds of four-to-the-floor two-chord magic unable to cast its spell over a public already too content with Ken Dodd and Hedgehoppers Anonymous.

The Sorrows battled to number 21 with their simpler lovesick blues similarly overwound in tempo like an amplified cardiac arrest, its drums pitter-pattering short of breath and a fuzzy riff throbbing like a ruptured artery. Five years represented an entire geological period in the infant evolution of rock'n'roll but Marc digs the contained panic of 'Take A Heart' as more than archaeology. Its sound registers like a prophetic storm warning to 'Two Little Boys' radio torpor, every shriek and squeal tapping out an urgent message. The dots and dashes aren't difficult for Marc to decode.

Make it loud.

Make it rhythmic.

Make it instant.

Make it *electric*.

NORTH OF THE BORDER, David is under siege by knitwear. Jumpers upon jumpers of chunky cable patterns and argyle diamonds blind his field of vision. Pickled accents slice the air between oaty coughs of accordion and homesick folky strums. He understands none of it and none of it understands him, but for the temporary posterity of soon-to-be-erased videotape and the outside chance of impressing the bedridden square-eyed of Speyside, he shakes his curls and sings his song about saying goodbye to London.

Strange young town.

Not as strange nor as cold as the old Granite City 500 miles north of Wardour Street where he blinks into the lens of an Aberdeen TV studio as the guest of *Cairngorm Ski Night*. It's the same couthy variety fare Grampian have been serving up on Friday and Saturday evenings since the station was founded a little over eight years ago. It's been *Aye Yours* and *Calum's Ceilidh*, but whatever the name the show remains the same bonnie sprig of low-cost and non-demanding cathode heather. The only distinguishing feature of *Cairngorm Ski Night* is the attempted illusion of an 'après-ski' shindig beamed from an Alpine lodge manned by the chosen host, Jimmy Spankie, presently stricken with a regrettable case of 'football ankle'. The obligatory woollens are provided by the invited audience from local skiing clubs, the regular music from the house bands and singers including 'the smiling voice of Grampian TV' himself, Dave McIntosh. This episode's special guests are gargantuan folkie Hamish Imlach, a bawdy twinkle in his eye and a gallon of moonshine sloshing around his gut, and David with his metropolitan moans that may or may not be suitable entertainment after a hard day's slaloming down the icy slopes of Glenshee.

He braves the North Sea winds for another night to play to students at the city's university, an event considered so obscure that the local press choose not to waste any pencil lead on this visit by the one-hit 'Space Oddity' star but focus all resources of reportage on the 'exotically dressed maidens' in grass skirts at a belly-dancing contest in Inverurie Town Hall. First prize, a fiver, is won by a girl from Tullynessle. Thirteen miles away, David Bowie comes, sings and goes without ceremony.

UNSURE WHERE TO TREAD, recorded sound blinks in the wilderness that is no longer 1969. There is still Radio Luxembourg on 208 and 247 metres of *won-der-ful* Radio 1. There are inky papers and colour magazines for girls, boys, pseuds, saps, bedroom movers and youth club groovers. But the television set is a pop tundra where the ready steady Sixties have got up and gone.

Hope faintly glimmers in a golden letter 'A' dangling on a chain around the neck of Ayshea, a beautiful doe-eyed 21-year-old Asian singer who's just been granted her own children's music show for Granada Television in Manchester. *Lift Off* is listed as 25 minutes of 'noise, dancing, dolly birds and flashing lights' straight after *Crossroads* on a Wednesday teatime. The show's producer is Muriel Young who publicly complains that 'television planners don't particularly like pop music'. The schedules are all the corroborating evidence she needs.

The BBC funnel their dislike of pop music into the Saturday night witching-hour wake of *Disco 2*. As in the kind of disco where people go not to dance but to self-embalm to the never-ending death rattle of 'Repent Walpurgis' by Procol Harum. Cryptkeeper-in-chief is Tommy Vance, bringing out the bodies of Hookfoot, Toe Fat and Blodwyn Pig between old hits accompanied by even older film clips, the closest *Disco 2*'s cobwebbed finger ever gets to a pop pulse.

Which leaves the merciful mother ship of *Top of the Pops*. Still the same Thursday night harem of syncopated female athleticism where the gals outnumber the guys 20 to one and lead the dance with wrists and ribcages pumping thin air like pistons, sending hips swivelling and spines flexing with sine waves of erotic potential. Jimmy Savile is host, just voted the year's favourite disc jockey by the readers of the *NME*. 'Who can keep up with the breezy, positive-thinking Jimmy?' Over there is a bug-eyed tramp with a flute twittering about witches while over here invaders from Northern Europe invoke the ancient goddess of love. Words of otherworldly wonder and worship are tempting the new superstars of the Seventies to claim their prize if only they would appear.

Until then, here's Edison Lighthouse. The first new number 1 of the decade is a human ventriloquist act. The dummies are a group called Greenfield Hammer, who as of last Christmas were gigging around Windsor for £20 a night. The hand up their backs belongs to young songwriter Tony Macaulay who needs to put faces to the record he's made with session singer Tony Burrows: a hummable pleasantry Macaulay wrote with Barry Mason and his wife Sylvan – 'Love Grows (Where My Rosemary Goes)'. Greenfield Hammer have the faces young enough to fit and the souls fickle enough to sell. The deal is that they promote the single with Burrows as their singer and change their name to Edison Lighthouse. The record has barely touched the shelves before they're gottle-o-geerin' on *Top of the Pops* in the second week of January. By the fourth, they're number 1.

The fakery is no secret, and when the secret is out a battle line is drawn which can never be erased. Pop music polarises. It started in late '69 when American cartoon band The Archies spent eight weeks at number 1, holding off The Beatles, Fleetwood Mac and David's 'Space Oddity' – a triumph of transparent artifice over perceived authenticity that heralded the outbreak of war between the snob at $33^1/_3$ and the libertine at 45, the sectarian bugle of elitist pomposity tooting a final solution against the snotty-faced scourge of commercial populism. And so pop becomes a partisan either/or. *Mirabelle* or *Melody Maker*. *Top of the Pops* or *Disco 2*. Tony Blackburn or Tommy Vance. Edison Lighthouse or Led Zeppelin.

With nothing and nobody in between.

IN BETWEEN and fully clothed, he lies under covers on a mattress on the floor of a bitterly cold stone terrace in Edinburgh. On one side, his bride-to-be, Angie. On the other, his former 'mime' teacher and occasional boyfriend Lindsay, as complete and unabridged a homosexual as nature dare manifest beyond the six-shilling pages of *Jeremy*. Both Angela and Lindsay understand their parallel intimate histories of the beautiful creature currently separating them and respectfully assume a friendly state of mutual truce. Not so much as a sock is removed and they snuggle as three innocent woodland babes in wintry hibernation.

Of puckish face and prancing theatrics, Lindsay is a mischievous pixie of a man. He possibly still sees David as Bosie to his Oscar but is decent enough to treat Angie as a woman of importance. David possesses plenty to go around between them but their appetites, though voracious, are not selfishly vulgar. They are both hopelessly in love with the boy, exchanging smiles like a secret handshake between two hearts corrupted by the same irresistible archangel.

'You too?'

'Of course.'

'Well, *look* at him.'

'Who *wouldn't*?'

Two years have passed since the older Lindsay fell for the younger David. First smitten by the voice as recorded on his debut album of jolly Jackanories about dreams, toys and silly boys, then the face from whence it came, then by slow degrees of backstage introductions and back-to-mine invitations to everything else that lay south. The pendulous spoils were all the more delicious for the knowledge that they'd almost been lost to a Tibetan monastery in the Scottish Borders where David was rashly considering consigning mind and body to the wasteful fate of Buddhist chastity. Lindsay took as much pride as pleasure in his mercy mission, which successfully convinced David that nirvana might be achieved through far more gratifying means than a day's lotus-positioned gibbering about flowers in Sanskrit.

Never one to give without receiving, David beseeched Lindsay to teach him the demonstrative art of 'mime' as he'd seen it performed by Lindsay himself in his Covent Garden pantomime inspired by Picasso's paintings of Pierrots and Harlequins. Lindsay eagerly instructed David as best he could in how to use his body as a tool of dramatic communication, how to enter, how to exit and how to enrapture an audience at all times between without saying a word. The master furthermore impressed upon his pupil the limitless powers of hair, costume and greasepaint. Before Lindsay, the stage had been merely a place where David could *be*. After Lindsay, it was the place he could *become*. Anything. Everything. A thousand new undiscovered selves awaiting at the dab of a powder puff and the snap of a leotard.

Under-skilled and over-eager, when let loose from Lindsay's Covent Garden dance studio with characteristic fancy-a-bit-of-that-ness, David began adding 'mime' artist to his official list of qualified talents. 'Mime', like music, was now something David did, all of the time. Music, he did reasonably well. 'Mime', he didn't. Lindsay grimaced, seizing the best of what David offered by inviting him into his theatre group for another of his pantomimes about clowns. On stage, *Pierrot in Turquoise* required David only to sing, leaving all dramatic postures and deft pirouettes to Lindsay and his half-blind dancing partner Jack, a shaven-headed Adonis who gave the impression of someone who came and went with three rubs of an Arabian lamp. Off stage, the show required David only to share Lindsay's bed, especially during its brief tour of the North when chauffeured by the production's female costume designer, Natasha. That she, too, had been regularly parking herself between David's sheets was a tryst he'd maintained in private for several weeks. Only when his appetites got the better of him one drizzly night in Cumbria did his shameful cat creep out of its bag with the thumping headboard and Natasha's satiated cries vibrating the walls of Lindsay's bed chamber, where he'd been lying prone and ready for identical service. The next morning, all pills and razorblades broke loose. A surface crybaby spurt from each wrist earned Lindsay only withering pity and surplus bandages from a local hospital. Natasha attempted a similarly half-hearted overdose. David wept, though whether for his thwarted libido or its victims was clear to none.

That was two years of endless other kisses-and-make-ups ago. Lindsay is now blissfully garreted in Edinburgh where he's invited David to perform in a dramatically revised version of *Pierrot in Turquoise* for the cameras of Scottish Television at their new colour studios converted from a former theatre. The dramatic revisions to Lindsay's old script add a subtitle, *The Looking Glass Murders*, and a new character, Columbine, played by a lithe young blonde named Annie. The plot, like the characters, is adapted from the centuries-old Italian traditions of the *commedia dell'arte* concerning the hapless Pierrot, his unfaithful Columbine and her lover Harlequin, once again played by the all-but-blind Jack. There is a bed, a flash of tit and arse and a terrifying display of cuckolded agony. All too transparent a ruse for Lindsay to turn his recurring suicidal histrionics over David's roving affections into half an hour's physical theatre.

Lindsay wants David to resume his voyeuristic minstrel's role as Cloud and to sing his favourite of David's old tunes – the ruby-slippered ballad 'When I Live My Dream' – but also demands new songs. David hasn't much time so dilutes 'London Bye Ta-Ta' with new words about a 'threepenny Pierrot' and prepares two half-hearted amorphous strums ready for when the STV cameras roll . . .

THIRTY-TWO DAYS into the new decade, the Sixties are dead and The Beatles a writ away from being buried with them. In a few days' time John Lennon will drop 'Instant Karma!' and Ringo will tell the papers he's considering calling his debut LP *Ringo Stardust*. Make a note, David. Old skins are shedding and new mornings breaking. *If you want it, here it is, come and get it.* You hear that, David? *But better hurry, Dave – it's going fast.* David? . . . David?

David, are you *there*?

No. David is not there. David is in Edinburgh, squatting on a stepladder wearing a nightie, his hair a fright wig, his face a pan-sticked boohoo, as three dancers leap around his feet in mounting hysterias of undress as part of a late-night 'mime' programme for Scottish Television.

This is how David Bowie spends the 32nd day of the Seventies.

FIVE

HE WALKS THROUGH the front double doors in his long black overcoat, feeling freer with every stride that takes him nearer the main gates at the bottom of the drive, like the shoots on the horse chestnuts already starting to harpoon through their sticky brown winter buds in rites-of-spring green. He continues along Brighton Road to the bus stop where he waits until the next northbound service takes him as far as Croydon. Time for a quick ciggie before the 194 departs. Through Shirley, West Wickham, Elmers End, then Beckenham, where he alights by the war memorial to finish his journey on foot. Up the hill, round the High Street, straight on over the railway bridge, past the station to where the houses grow bigger and further apart. He's done the same route many times before and as he crosses over into Southend Road his heart is beating. Then he sees it through the trees, the unmistakable jut of its weathervaned spire. A few more steps. The push of a doorbell. A short wait. A turn of a bolt and there he is.

Little brother.

The day is an unanchored blur that passes much too fast. Coffee, cigarettes, records and books. He is shown things and played things which he half-reads and half-hears. He is there and not there. He is fed and he is asked questions which he tries to answer with the part of himself who *is* there, and when he does so, he begins to think that perhaps he is more

37

actually there than he first believed. But there is still that missing part stuck in quicksand, fingertips twitching above the surface, which nobody wants to rescue. More smoke and more music. He hums. He half-sings. There are jokes. He laughs. He can still laugh. Little brother always makes him laugh.

He's famous now, little brother. He likes to tell people back *there*. Sometimes they look at him like they don't believe him, but it's true, and he can prove it. He called him a 'genius' once. He's even had his name in *Jackie*.

Who has influenced you most?
> Go on, tell 'em, David.

'My brother Terry.'
> Brother, he said.
> Full brother, not half.

'He's seven years older than I am.'
> He's almost ten.

'I'm 22 now, he's 29.'
> He's 32.

'He was very keen on jazz when I was at a very impressionable age, and that led me into it.'
> A love supreme.

'I idolised John Coltrane and Eric Dolphy and learned to play the clarinet and tenor saxophone when I was 12. When I first came into the business six years ago it was as a jazz musician.'
> Was it?

'Terry was very bohemian . . .'
> And still is.

'. . . and introduced me to the writing that meant a lot to him – like Jack Kerouac and Allen Ginsberg.'
> Who saw the best minds of his generation destroyed by madness.

'And all this led me into songwriting.'
> Uh . . .

And all that led him into songwriting, he says. Only he forgot to tell them where it led Terry. That's the funny part. That's the best punchline of all. See, because *he* ends up in *Jackie* magazine and Terry ends up in The Cane.

Why didn't he tell them?

My brother Terry? Well, he's off his gourd! They had to put him in The Cane for his own good. Y'know, The Cane? It's where they send you when you lose your marbles. You'll hear it in every playground round here. 'Watch it, sonny, or you'll be up The Cane.' Cos that's where Coltrane, Dolphy, Kerouac and Ginsberg got Terry, mate. Up The Cane without a fucking paddle!

The sun has moved so far in the sky its light can no longer be seen. Little brother says it's time to go. He says he'll drive him back to the bus stop down the road to save him walking. They'll take the big van and his friends John and Roger can come along for the ride. The genius doesn't want to go. Knowing he must, he buttons up his long dark coat that makes him look like he's in the Gestapo and climbs into the van.

The drive is short. He sits in the back like a pet amphibian blinking in its tank at a world removed. When they reach the stop there is no queue and the bus isn't for another ten minutes. Little brother and his friends with strange accents say goodbye. He waits, watching their van turn the corner and drive out of sight. Then, hands in pockets to keep warm from the cold, he marches over to the warm light of liberty glowing from The Bricklayers Arms.

He has no plan, only a will not to return. Or perhaps half a plan. Sit it out. Miss his bus. Walk back to little brother's house and ask if he can stay until morning. One without lather queues, distant screams and dribbling prunes in the cafeteria.

He walks to the bar, leans with one elbow taking his weight. A flawless performance of an ordinary bloke ordering a pint.

He asks.

It's pulled.

He pays.

He sips.

The sweet taste of normality. He pulls out a cigarette, puts it in his mouth, scrabbles in his pocket for matches, fingers rattling out an almost empty box, strikes, ignites and sucks hard. A man alone with a beer and a cigarette. He wants to savour each second for all the sanity he can, praying the ground won't spit fire and the sky won't rip open before he reaches the bottom of the glass. Please God, just let him be.

'Terry!'

The sky rips. Little brother and his friends have found him. They've been to the Wimpy bar. When they came out they drove back past the bus stop and didn't see him in the queue. The bus was still due. But, little brother, he said he knew where he'd be. And he was right. Here he is.

'Oh. Hiya, David.'

Little brother doesn't look pleased to see him. 'You'll miss your bus.'

'Oh?' He cradles his glass. 'I'm just having a pint.'

He will not be rushed. His sips become slower and ceremonial. Another cigarette and every suck, every second becomes more precious than the last, knowing that when the glass is emptied and the ashtray fed there is nothing but a bed in Blake ward and the shortening of the ten miles that lie between.

Outside, the bus has been and gone. Little brother says he'll have to drive him back, which is what he feared. The friends, John and Roger, don't know where 'back' is but stay along for the ride. John sits in the back of the van beside him. Little brother drives in thundery silence but John fills the air with his cheery flat vowels about nothing and everything. He asks John where he's from. He's told 'Hull'. A cog turns and he starts listing aloud the forward line of Hull City AFC.

'Ken Houghton . . . Ken Wagstaff . . . Chris Chilton.'

John is chuffed that anyone down here would know the First Eleven of his local Division Two squad. But there aren't enough subs on the Tigers' bench to fill the conversational void all the way. A carousel of streetlights glides over the windscreen, each streak of yellow sodium a link in the chain reeling him back. He sees the driveway before anyone else, and when the van slows down and turns to follow its bend he looks into his lap rather than at the pale ward lights through the barbed-wire silhouettes of leafless trees.

The building looms like a monster carved out of the night itself. The van stops. A 'goodbye' is mumbled and out he clambers.

Then he turns and steals a fleeting glance at little brother in the driving seat. Little *half*-brother. It's hopeless to pretend otherwise. Their builds are similar, even if he's older and heavier, but their faces are unalike. They are two sons of two distinctly different fathers.

He is a Rosenberg. Swarthy Gallic features, prominent ears and blue eyes that ought to sparkle more than his fate allows. It's a handsome face, or would be if somebody knew how to plug him in and switch it on.

Whereas little brother, he's a Jones. Haywood Stenton's doppelgänger. Dead man walking. The same chopstick bones, skeletal cheeks, matinee-idol chin, his winged ears, pinched nose, sparing lips and taut philtrum, the rolling forehead, and the smile that could be a grimace, his gaze that fell not *on* but *through* someone, the same outward laugh and inward shiver. The man everyone knew as John Jones had the cool, economical face of someone who might be a Nobel-winning rocket scientist or a serial poisoner. His son has that face. The exact same face. Only the eyes, uniquely warped through nurture to spite nature, are different. The eyes that meet his now for a fraction of a second. A fraction too short to telegraph a lifetime's distress signals. A look that finds no words in its ricochet of sorrow, fear, loneliness and regret. Just echoes.

And all this . . .

   And all this led me into . . .

      And all this led me into all this . . .

He hears the van pull away as he steps up the granite steps of the madhouse leading him into a yackety-yakking screaming vomiting concrete void of hellfire, piss, metallic tea, carbolic soap – and all this. He has no heart to wonder what little brother will tell the others about where this is and why he took him back here, or whether they're already talking about him, or whether they're travelling home in silence, working it out for themselves until the day should come when the closed book behind the steering wheel chooses to flip open its pages and tell them all this about the person who has influenced him the most.

In Blake, the floors are the same polished brown, the curtains orange, his blanket green. Tomorrow there will be another lather queue, sponge and custard, lounges full of faraway stares, a crossword, a game of cards, pills to swallow and another strangled echo of some poor sod being straitjacketed on Salter. He takes to his bed amid a grainy darkness of coughs, creaks and stifled moans. Eyes closed, he sucks hard on the taste of bitter on his tongue and falls asleep in The Bricklayers Arms.

THE KILLING TOOK three minutes. The trial takes 12 days. The jury take six hours. Four teenage boys from Roehampton: an 18-year-old butcher, a 16-year-old wood carver's apprentice and two schoolboys, both 15. Guilty.

It wasn't murder to them, nor to the eight other teenagers from the Alton Estate who stood and watched and cheered and laughed as they beat a man to death with fence palings as he crawled on his hands and knees trying to get away from them. His name was Michael de Gruchy. A 29-year-old clerk at a solicitor's firm in Moorgate, he lived in Mitcham with his recently widowed mother. On a Thursday night last September, Michael drove his dark-green Austin 1100 to a leafy corner of SW15 where he parked sometime after 9 p.m. Slightly drunk, wearing a black leather jacket, he walked to the subway under the A3 near Putney Vale Cemetery that led to Wimbledon Common. They were waiting for him. Not necessarily him, Michael. Just any one of *them*.

They didn't *want* to kill him. So one of the boys who repeatedly kicked him in the face said in court when asked how Michael died of lacerations to the brain and a fractured skull. He was still just about alive when he was found lying on the pavement by passers-by. At first they thought he must be drunk. They asked if he needed the police. He slurred and begged to be left alone but a motorist called an ambulance. Two hours later, Michael was pronounced dead in a hospital less than a mile away.

Beating them or robbing them. Queer bashing or queer rolling. The 68-year-old judge was unfamiliar with the terms and asked one of the girls in the gang to clarify.

'Bashing means going around beating up queers.'

'And queer rolling?'

'It's bloody well all the same!'

M'lud was not impressed. He sends the four who did it to prison, the eldest to life, and the eight who watched to borstal. Brave little queer bashers who'll soon be forced to jerk off or suck off, or be tied down face down as warders turn blind eyes or wait their turn.

The tabloids rustle with disgust but more for the cause than the crime. The sordid horror stories of what happens on Wimbledon Common when normal God-fearing folk are tucked up in bed. 'The headquarters of a sadistic homosexual secret society' bellows the *Sun*, shuddering at the scourge of decency known as 'The Leather Queens'; all dressed in identical black jackets, calf-length boots, jeans and 'white jumpers', they congregate for orgies by Queensmere Pond where they 'whip each other naked', sometimes 'up to 300 at a time'. Every word, Fleet Street gospel.

A plucky broadsheet hound braves the depths of the estate where anonymous Kids A and B tell it like it is.

Kid A: *'When you're hitting a queer you don't think you're doing wrong, you think you're doing good. If you want money off a queer then you get it off him – there's nothing to be scared of because you know they won't go to the law.'*

Kid B: *'In the old days we used to be satisfied with smashing up their cars. That's why de Gruchy parked his car so far away. They used to drive up there in their city suits and change into their leathers and go over the Common.'*

Kid A: *'If there was a queer taking my brother, I'd smash his head in with a brick. To paste. I'd enjoy it.'*

Kid B: *'There was one, I had a big log and I smashed him and he fell down and yelled "Help, help, help" and we all ran away. Once you've beaten one pansy queer you get confident and you're not scared any more and you beat them all up.'*

Kid A: *'We beat up blokes and you know they're queer. I don't want some bloke screwing me. It's like the kids in West London and the Pakis. I hate them. I don't understand them. That's it.'*

It's bloody well all the same.

The families are quick to protest their innocence. 'Something must be done to save our children from the perverts of Wimbledon Common,' rages the father of one of the killers. 'Many of the children on the estate have been molested by these odd people. This is why queer bashing started.'

The reverend in charge of the local youth club offers admonishing comfort from above. 'These boys are not wicked,' he sermonises. 'In a terrible sort of way they thought they were doing a public service.'

England, 1970. Hear the Word of the Lord.

DIFFERENT YOUTHS, different clubs. Nine miles south-east of the killing fields of Wimbledon, David's friends found more pleasant pastimes. It began as just another folk club in the back of The Three Tuns, a large Tudor-beamed pub on Beckenham High Street. Six months on, it was now an Arts Lab. The main distinction between a folk club and an Arts Lab being that one was where people went to hear second-rate Simon & Garfunkel and the other to build the foundation of a new Utopia. One of self-sufficiency, autonomy, love and liberty: where everyone worked as one in communal cooperative bliss, where neighbours would pull up the plain grey paving slabs outside their houses to replace them with bright pinks and blues as beautiful byways of a revolutionary new society. That, and a place where the fabulous freaks of the South-East could congregate every Sunday for music, poetry, laughter, irreverence, joy and absurdity in their self-made stoner Shangri-La.

Beckenham Arts Lab refocused David's centre of gravity from WC1 and all its disappointments to the wild frontier of BR3. Here he was free to trial any raw acoustic first drafts he pleased between the wry bedsit rags of Keith Christmas, the cacophonous thunks of Cliff Penge and the SE20s, and anyone else with the guts and guitar to stand up and stutter blank verse, or sing 'Suzanne' in front of a hundred or more hippies, radicals, communists, anarchists, *IT* girls, *Oz* boys, students, squatters, strugglers and reality jugglers.

But six months on, all is still the same. Too much the same. The room is the same, the oil lamps are the same: the bodies in the audience, their clothes and haircuts, long and brown and denim and florally, the smell of tobacco and incense and last night's resin, the faces behind the microphone and the songs they sing and the tight jumpers and saggy jeans they wear, the poems they recite and the mumbled introductions and bashful thank yous and the polite applause, the girls giggling as they stroke shiny ribbons of Sea Witched hair from their wanton eyes and the fingers wiping beer from moustaches on faces too young to sprout them, the stickiness of the chequered carpet and the surreal ordinariness of the flock wallpaper. Everything and everyone. It's all the fucking same.

The laboratory has become laborious and the experimentation has stopped. The happening no longer is, and in its stagnation the same gravity which once held David fast to its stage as a captain to his wheel has weakened. His withdrawal is gradual, but his course is fixed. Abandon ship.

In Haddon Hall his mind's lifeboat bobs adrift, flicking the pages of that week's *Melody Maker*. There's no escape from Led Zeppelin these days and here they are again, a photo of David's old Sixties session mate Jimmy Page on the cover. 'The Paganini of the Seventies' the *Maker* call him. 'British groups have already kicked off the New Year with a massive blitz on the American market,' it says. British groups. Nothing about British singers.

He floats on to the classifieds. There's the Marquee house ad listing his show the following week. 'David Bowie'. A relief after *Time Out* listed him as 'David Berry'. The rest of the Marquee calendar, again, is mainly groups. The Groundhogs. Daddy Long Legs. Sweet Water Canal. The Time Box. Rare Bird. Toast. All the other live ads too. Deep Purple. Mott The Hoople. All groups. And most of the groups just have one word names like Toast.

Taste.

Yes.

Spirit.

Family.

Free.

Spice.

Fire.

Screw.

Heaven.

Smoke.

Bottle.

Smile.

Egg.

There is himself, there is Keef Hartley, there is Al Stewart and there is John & Beverley Martyn. Everything else is Egg on Toast. So many groups that even the shiny girls' weeklies *Jackie* and *Mirabelle* are devoting pin-up pages to unbarbered uglies like Ten Years After.

David has no group. He has only regular players. He has Tony joining him on bass and faithful John on drums. Sometimes he has Tim, the guitarist in John's band Junior's Eyes. But it's never the same from one gig to the next. Sometimes he's joined by all of them. Sometimes a few. Sometimes none. And however many people are on stage, one or four, the name on the poster is still David Bowie. Except when misprinted as David Berry.

The dry land on his horizon – *an idea* – he needs a band and he needs his band to be a group. A proper four-piece with a snappy one-word name like Kapow or Zap or Wow. He has one ready and waiting in Tony, John and Tim. Only now that Junior's Eyes have decided to split after their next gig supporting David, Tim's already thrown his pick in the ring with Terry Reid's Fantasia. Which leaves David without a regular guitar player. In the rock'n'roll trenches of 1970, no group can be a group without one.

What he needs is his own Page. A virtuoso. A master of melodic caprice who can embellish the blank spaces above, below and between voice, thud and bomp with white-hot semiquavers bent and twisted into rococo curls of amplified sound. The question is who?

LEAD GUITARIST. Gibson.
Seeks pro or semi-pro group.
Creative. Own material . . .

'Own material'? Jesus, no. David isn't going to find them in the small-print two-bob chancers in the *Maker* classifieds.

Who, though?

Names ricochet off his living-room wall. David is listening to Tony list possibles and maybes from his recent work memory. Each is met by a cautious nod or shake of the head. The vacancy stays open and the search continues.

Who?

'I know someone.'

A familiar voice pipes up from the corner of the room where John has been listening. At first they don't flinch.

'My mate in Hull.'

Now they do. Tony's eyes tell John he's being a nuisance. John ignores them.

'Honest. He's a dead-good player. Jeff Beck, Hendrix – he does all sorts.'

David's attention is won.

'I'm going back this weekend. I can bring him back down with me in the car.'

An eyebrow cocks and a cigarette smoulders.

'Just try him out, see what he's like, and if you don't think he's any good I'll take him back. Just to give him a go, like.'

David scratches the corner of his mouth. 'Your mate?'

'Yeah.'

'From Hull?'

'Yeah.'

David looks at Tony. A shrug. A smirk. Then turns back to John. 'This mate of yours – what's his name?'

SIX

A STRANGE END-OF-THE-LINE CITY with its own strange end-of-the-line smell. Led blindfold through its streets, anyone who'd ever smelled it before would know by the familiar sour taste at the back of their throat where they were. The locals, they say it's emissions from the cocoa factory wafting on the northerly wind. But no cocoa ever tasted like the buried-alive odour of Hull.

The city's proper name is Kingston; Hull, the river upon which it squats on the north bank of the Humber Estuary as it droops down into the sea. But Hull is no King's Town. Hull is as Hullishly Hull a place as the combined efforts of industry, the Luftwaffe and a polio epidemic could ever sculpt from steel, bomb and skin pallor. Its streets are flat, its accent flatter and its colour palette a spectrum of browns and greys where even the phone boxes are a bled-to-death white. Hull is like nowhere else and nowhere else has ever wanted to be Hull. There are days of grey-skied, cobble-damp, cocoa-choked Hullishness when even Hull isn't so sure it does either.

Nowhere is all Mick has ever known. He is Hull-born and to Hull's turf bound; at the age of 23 a mower of its grass, a painter of its pitches and a digger of its flowerbeds. This is not his choice but he chooses to accept the pittance luck has provided for him having once dreamed, many times tried and too often failed. From anywhere else, he might be bitter. But he is Hull's own Michael Ronson, raised to keep his sleepy blue eyes on the gutter rather than tempt disappointment by ever looking up at any stars.

Rake in hand, he is Prince Charming in reverse, a handsome blond Viking with Claudette Colbert lashes and the softest of accents made to whisper wooing poetry up at balconies. The rightful belle of the ball made Cinderella of civic maintenance. He digs the soil, empties the barrow and prunes the hedges with hands that have the power to shake new constellations among the heavens. He has earth where he wants electricity, blades where he needs frets, and the tuneless hum of a petrol motor where he should be filling the dreadnought Humber skies with notes detonating like fireworks. Such things are not considered tragic round here. This is merely how fortune favours the bright lights of Hull. One day Tin Pan Alley, the next Preston Road.

Mick's church is Jesus Christ of Latter-Day Saints but his religion is music. He can read and write it, play piano, fiddle and recorder. A cautious kid, he was quick to discover carrying a violin case is a valentine to danger when you live on the Greatfield Estate. Until destiny, in the siren's twang of rock'n'roll, found him, saved him and placed an electric guitar between his fingers.

Baptised by Duane Eddy and Hank Marvin, Mick served his apprenticeship in village halls, backrooms and ballrooms amid the swarm of Transit-vanned Chuck-Berryisms buzzing over the East Riding. In the Flat Earth stretching from the Beverley Regal to the Kon-Tiki Club, from the rails of fab gear in Royce's to the Gondola café, Mick was a star. But there only. Daring to dwell beyond the horizon of the local Skyline Ballroom, in the World Cup summer of '66, smelling glory in the breeze, 19-year-old Mick tempted fate. Handing in his notice as a Co-op delivery man, guitar in hand, he galloped south.

Harlow was not London, but the bed and board of a family friend offered a close enough stepping stone roughly a half-hour's train ride away. Closer than the racks of Stardisc, Sydney Scarborough or the listening booths in Hammonds department store where vinylite meteorites were treasured and traded as exotic evidence of intelligent life on an unreachably distant planet.

London was reassuringly alien, unfathomably big, bewilderingly fast, dazzlingly bright and dizzyingly loud, Mick just another infinitesimal atom of disoriented humanity smashing between its streetlights. He sought refuge from chaos in the classifieds of music papers and lonely cups of coffee steaming up Soho windows, squeaking spyholes in their condensation to watch the world with no need for him shimmying by. Dressing the part, he cut his hair to fit West End fashion in the daily-dwindling hope his role would come up. He thought it had when he found himself playing lead in a group of psychedelic wastrels who'd managed to secure finance and a luxurious residence in a Mayfair townhouse in return for surrendering their minds to a Scientology splinter cult. A weekly retainer allowed Mick to stop the Essex commute and take new lodgings in Primrose Hill while promises of a management deal with Donovan hitman Mickie Most and a spot on *Ready Steady Go!* were enough to dissuade nagging doubts over his paymasters' doomsday prophecies. Until the day the rest of the group and their Nostradamus-in-chief upped and vanished to the Bahamas to ramp up preparations for the looming apocalypse. Leaving Mick in London where his had already begun.

For bread he took a daytime job as a garage mechanic, and for need of keeping the dream alive, threw himself into the first group who'd take him. Neither could lift his spirits, now fading faster than the yellowing leaves of his first metropolitan autumn. The other side of the tracks from his Gloucester Avenue digs, an old circular Victorian railway shed was about to reopen as a new arts venue with the launch of the *International Times*. Across town in Chelsea and Mayfair, Antonioni was pulling focus on the last frames of *Blowup*. The capital was approaching full Sixties swing and Mick was motion-sick. His choice was as stark as the new number 1 from the Small Faces: 'All Or Nothing'. Mick bought a one-way ticket home to nothing. By the time his prodigal boots touched Hull tarmac again Jim Reeves was top of the charts. Life had taken two steps further back than before he left.

The security of a job in a paint factory was the 'ordinary and simple life' he'd been fool enough to fantasise about in letters home. London had beaten but not entirely broken him, and what shards of ambition were still there waiting to be stuck back together found necessary glue in a local R&B band similarly scarred by three years of dashed hopes, deserting members and two failed singles on the same label as The Dave Clark Five.

Captained by the hairy chin and hairier voice of Benny Marshall, The Rats were a sinking ship who needed Mick in their mischief just as much as he needed them: he, their Hendrix; they, his Experience. The Rats now played Jimi, Cream and Moby Grape. Mick played these and everything else according to the teachings of his new prophet, Jeff Beck of Latter-Day Yardbirds. It was the squeals of delight on 'Over Under Sideways Down', what Mick called 'that violin guitar sound', that did it. After Beck, Mick needed look and listen no further, converted to a life of imitation as the sincerest form of flattery.

Three years unthreaded without distinction. Days killing time on the shop floor; nights of roll-ups and pints of black velvet, subbing cider for champers; weekends topping the bill above Scarborough rivals The Mandrakes and their too-smooth Allen Palmer; screams, schoolgirls, roadside cafés and rattling axles in quiet lay-bys. Only sometimes would an old upright piano in the corner of a church hall stir a chance tinkle of 'Für Elise' between unloading the gear – the revelation of a secret maestro's talents untapped. So they'd remain.

The Rats made new recordings, but never new records. They tried changing their name to The Treacle. They changed drummers and bass players, cover versions and stage clothes. But nothing ever changed for The Rats, nor Mick, except for girls and guitars.

A home game Saturday in the winter of '68. As Tigers supporters were sloshing out of Boothferry Park cheated by their 3–3 draw with Cardiff City, over on Spring Bank at Cornell's Music Shop providence bartered. Mick traded in his blond Telecaster part-exchange for a new black Les Paul Custom. He took it straight to a Treacle gig that night at a school in Melton, a few miles west of Hull, where he broke it in live on stage. Later, he decided to amend the frets, and the colour, stripping the black finish from the body to reveal the natural maple underneath. Under stage lights, the varnished wood glinted gold. Jason had found his fleece.

All else was shipwrecked flotsam. A new job gardening for the city council. A teenage girlfriend. Another gig in an East Hull secondary modern. But once savagely bitten by London, Mick was twice as shy of ever returning. It was miracle enough that his Greatfield neighbour, Michael Chapman, a local singer-songwriter anchored to the city despite a record deal with EMI's new progressive label, Harvest, convinced him to book time off to come and play guitar on his next album. Mick spent four days in a basement studio in Denmark Street living the dream which three years earlier had eluded him. The following week he was back behind his mower. Chapman couldn't understand why Mick wouldn't leave The Rats and join his touring band instead. There was no mystery as far as Mick could see. He had his guitar, his band, his job, his Denise, his world, his Hull. It wasn't the good life, but it was a life good enough.

So he keeps telling himself. A life good enough. Even this parky winter's morning: thick socks, trousers tucked inside his wellies, navy donkey jacket buttoned tight.

Where's it to be today?

Sports pitches up Andrew Marvell School. Need the lines remarking. Whole bloody lot. Brown creosote, cheaper than paint. Fill up the wheel-to-wheel and off he trundles: one man, his machine and the secret symphonies inside his head. The lines steadily unravel on frosty turf, the creosote filling his nostrils; private melodies pinball between his ears, blocking out the squeak of the marker wheel, the distant cars, the odd cawing gull, the faint cry of someone shouting.

'Mick!'

Music, squeak, gull, car, shout.

'Mick!'

Squeak, music, car, shout, gull.

'Mick!'

Gull, squeak, shout, music, car.

'*Mick!*'

Car, shout, music, gull, squeak.

'*Mick!*'

HE STOPS. He turns and sees a figure walking towards him across the grass.

'Mick!'

Mick recognises him. A former fellow Rat.

'Oh! Hiya, John.'

Funny, though. Last he heard John was in London.

'What the hell are *you* doing here?'

★

HE WANTED TO BE A BEATLE or a Stone, and so given the chance at the age of 15 he became a Gonk. His first band, his first drum kit. The Big Time was the Regal ballroom, bottom of a local bill of East Riding rhythm and Beverley blues. That's when John Cambridge first met the older kid from The Crestas with the blond guitar to match his hair. A star in shrink-wrap.

Sixteen, restless and gonked out, John answered an ad in *Melody Maker* placed by an unnamed 'Professional Group' seeking a new drummer. The Hullaballoos, from Hull, were English nobodies who'd fooled America into thinking they were somebodies on the coat-tails of the British Invasion thanks to investment from the eccentric squire of the East Riding's largest stately home. Passing his audition, John found a new best mate in the group's other recent recruit, Mick Wayne, a singer and guitarist from Surbiton who happily swapped his malnourished existence in a bedsit behind Hull's Albert Avenue swimming baths for the free bed and board of John's mam and dad.

All too soon The Hullaballoos split up and Wayne moved back down south. But his gratitude to John was a debt he'd one day repay: their friendship, the first tether of future legend.

The Sixties Humber beat went on. John followed it the best he could in the elementary soul of a group named after a local cinema, ABC. Fate following its own tempo, a better offer soon came across the table of the Gondola café from the blond kid who'd once been a Cresta before vanishing to London. Now home again, Mick Ronson asked John if he wanted to join The Rats. Another tether firmly pegged.

Ronson replaced Wayne as the new Mick in John's life: friend, bandmate and co-writer of a slightlydelic Rats original about the death of a coalman: 'The Rise And Fall Of Bernie Gripplestone'. John took the 'Gripplestone' from Lennon's Gripweed in *How I Won the War*, Mick, 'The Rise And Fall' from The Shadows' 'Flingel Bunt'. The Rats recorded it for posterity at a home studio just off a local country stretch called Great Gutter Lane. Fate echoing the location, the song washed into oblivion.

It was John who in '68 encouraged The Rats to rebrand themselves The Treacle, but it was as the reverted Rats that they sacked him the following spring. Given the choice between an extra day's rehearsal and darts, John chose darts. He agreed they'd be better to find another drummer, and said his goodbyes after his last practice in a hall outside Hull in a village called Woodmansey. Such is destiny and its twisted sense of humour.

The oche didn't have John for long before his old Hullaballoos saviour Mick Wayne reappeared, inviting him to see his new group, a heavy noise called Junior's Eyes, up from London to play a gig in Scarborough. By the end of the gig John was coerced on stage to jam. Three days later, he became their new drummer.

The job meant seven pounds 50 a week and swapping his bed in Hull for a mattress on the floor of a garage in a Marylebone mews sharing with the band's guitarist, Tim, and their Australian roadie, Roger. The band had already recorded a debut album with John's predecessor, *Battersea Power Station*, produced by Tony Visconti and released the same month Mick Wayne earned some overtime as a session player at Trident on a song about a doomed astronaut named Major Tom. Wayne played its slide guitar solo using a Ronson brand cigarette lighter. The strangest of stars were aligning.

It was Tony who'd recommended Wayne, even though he never produced 'Space Oddity', so when it came to make the rest of David's album Tony hired him again, this time inviting the rest of Wayne's group. Which is how Junior's Eyes became David's band and Hull's John Cambridge became David's drummer. And how, many months later, under the moulded ceilings of Haddon Hall, David Bowie first heard the name of Mick Ronson from the lips of John as he struggled to persuade him he had a friend in Hull who was good enough to be his new guitar player.

And why John's been driving around East Hull all morning looking for him. Bilton, Longhill, searching for the council gardeners' portable wooden hut where Mick usually takes his tea breaks. When he finds it, Mick isn't there, but his mate Trevor is.

'Mick? He's up Andrew Marvell. Rugby pitches.'

Andrew Marvell. Rugby pitches. Just up the road.

That's him! And he would have to be right over the other side on the furthest bloody rugby pitch, wouldn't he?

'Mick . . .'

'WHAT THE HELL are *you* doing here?'

Mick asks, so John tells him. Junior's Eyes are packing it in and he's now drumming solely for David Bowie. The bloke who did 'Space Oddity'.

Mick listens, still pushing the line marker leaving its steady slug trail of brown behind him, John keeping pace.

David needs a guitar player. That's why he's here. To ask Mick if he's interested.

'Ah . . . uh . . . no.'

It comes with a shake of the head and an unbroken stride. The wheel squeaks and the creosote streaks. Mick keeps pushing the machine. John sticks with him.

He tries again. David Bowie. London. Gigs. Making records. Money. Somewhere to stay.

'Me? No.'

Fuck's sake! David bloody Bowie. 'Space Oddity'. Top 10. A gig at the Marquee this week. Just come down and meet him. Free lift. Free board. Nothing to lose.

'Ah . . . ur . . .'

The whimper of the scalded once but scalded deep. No, not again. Not that London again. That recent thing with Michael Chapman, well, that was only a few days. But that was enough.

'Nah.'

Mick turns a sharp 90 degrees. John follows. He will not give up because he cannot give up. He is now a puppet of history and if he doesn't dance to the pull of its strings then time will buckle, spotlights will fade, galaxies go undiscovered and their stars not shine, dance floors will empty, transistors fall silent, graffiti go unscribbled, loves not speak their name, heroes and heroines not rise from council slumber, lifestyles be stillborn and identities lost in lipsticks untwisted, art will go unhung, screens be blank, clothes rails be colourless, movements not move, revolutions not spark, souls never mate and a trillion unspent orgasms of teenage mind and body will perish in cold cumless genocide.

All this at stake and not a single thunderbolt zappazapping from the skies willing Mick to think. Mick, just *think*!

The wheel stops. His pitches are finished, their lines marked out perfectly. Yet John is still here, still talking about a job going in London with this David Bowie fella.

London?

The word tugs at his heart like the chain of a ship's anchor. And leave Hull again? Leave his Rats? Leave 8 Milton Grove, mam, dad, little Maggi and David? Leave Denise, engagement rings and duty's binding? Leave Carr Lane, Whitefriargate and Land Of Green Ginger? Leave foul cocoa winds, grey skies and creosote? Leave disappointment? Leave frustration? Leave anger? Leave fear? Leave never leaving?

'Come on,' says John and the heavens hold their breath. Mick catches his. Then moves his lips.

'Ah . . .

      . . .

        . . .

          . . .

            . . .

              . . .

                . . .

                  . . .

                    . . . Go on then.'

SEVEN

THE LIME-GREEN, CREAM-ROOFED Hillman Minx, YWF 67, turns off Wardour Street, parking in the little alley behind the Marquee club. The rest of John's band are already inside setting up where Mick follows, sizing up the famous striped stage and the black empty void in front, remembering the few times he set wishful foot here during his lost lonely London of '66. Junior's Eyes ready their gear for tonight's last hurrah: a longer evening ahead for John and their guitarist Tim, who will be playing two sets, the second backing David.

Night drapes, the doors open and long hair sails in on an armada of tight hips and baggy bottoms. Junior's Eyes open wide and close for good before the new David Bowie band slice sunlight through their heavy wake. Mick's attentions flit around the stage from Tim's fret fingers to those of the 12-string man-maiden behind the mic. He likes what he hears: songs with melodies that shift chords with confidence, *musical* music with soft edges that could do with some hardening. And what he sees: a singer who *sings*, a voice that soars, a face that wants it and a body that gets it. David is serious. This much, Mick can tell.

They've yet to be introduced. It doesn't happen before the gig in the backstage tension of too-occupied minds, nor in the immediate aftermath as adrenaline is unplugged with leads and equipment, boxed up and shipped out in slo-mo reflections. It doesn't happen in the Marquee at all, where the bar is soft and liquor absent, but a few doors down in the licensed drinking club above a Soho bookmakers, La Chasse. The Hunt. It is only then, when David ceases to be David Bowie of spotlit mystique and becomes John's mate, Dave, that he bothers to speak to the blond northerner standing in his midst. But it's still not much of a conversation. Post-show, David hasn't the strength to be more than civil and Mick is meekly Hullish to a fault.

It takes a change of scene, and language, before these polar spirits of north and south properly fuse. The scene, the spectral time before bed in Haddon Hall where Mick will spend the night on the living-room floor with John and Roger. The language, music. One to one with acoustic guitars, Mick finally says everything in fingers and strings that he can't with lips and words. It is then David stops and listens. There, in the very room where not one week earlier David and Tony sat silently braying like disbelieving jackasses when John tried to tell them their intended Chosen One was alive and well, if just about living, in a distant town one vowel from Hell. The seraph of sound who sits here now, watching David's frets, ears and eyes following the chords, embroidering their density with gentle curlicues and graceful volutes. Mick is all instinct, wits and harmonies. He doesn't play along. He tunes in. He conjoins. He listens for the spaces David doesn't know are there, hoisting silvery light from out of their silent depths.

Last night's waking dream becomes broad daylight's reality as Mick raises his lids to find he's still in a wonderland of high ceilings, stone arches and stained glass vibrating to the echo of nearby American voices. All risen by lunchtime, David resumes their stringed dialogue. It's just another jam for Mick, but John knows David well enough to read the dumb wonder in his eyes and sees his mission accomplished. Tony, too, is a portrait of mute awe. Angie's blessing is a little less discreet. In Mick's face she sees a canvas itching for paint and in his playing hears the cries of Carnegie Hall. He is beautiful, talented, sweet-natured, willing and very able. She tells David what he already knows. Mick's his guy.

David knows, but he isn't certain Mick does. The only way to find out is an initiation ceremony and he has such a rite that week to hand. Baptism by fire of radio. Today is Wednesday and tomorrow David is to record a concert before a live audience to be broadcast three days later by the BBC. He'll play some of it solo, the rest backed by John and Tony, but he still needs a guitar player. He asks Mick to join him, on stage and on air. A chance for David to gauge the true measure of the heart that pumps beneath the feathery voice and camel lashes.

Mick hears David say 'radio' and his skull hums with the heat overload of every trannie in every bedroom from Bransholme to Gipsyville buzzing with the caress of his fingers. Less than 24 hours since they've met and only another 24 hours before the gig without any formal band rehearsal, Mick would be a madman to say yes and an idiot to say no. To David's delight he pleads insanity.

'THIS AFTERNOON'S PROGRAMME, we have David Bowie who's famed in hit parade circles for one of last year's best records, "Space Oddity".'

The voice belongs to Marc's friend Peel, addressing the seated audience in the BBC's Paris Theatre, just down the road from Broadcasting House. 'This afternoon's programme' is a Thursday evening concert recorded for this coming weekend's *The Sunday Show*. Or, as Peel likes to think of it, 'a sort of groovy Radio 1 club'.

'He'll be joined a little later in the programme by a horde of musicians, and I'll be telling you about that when it comes.'

It comes after four solo songs, then another two with Tony and John.

'On this next number, in addition to John Cambridge on drums and Tony Visconti on bass – and, of course, David on guitar – we have Mick Ronson who'll be playing lead guitar . . .'

And the Humber becomes electric.

'. . . who's recorded on Michael Chapman LPs – those of you who've heard Michael Chapman's LPs, he's one of my favourite singers . . .'

And from this minute in history, now obsolete.

Nobody has heard the LP, singular, Mick recorded with Michael Chapman called *Fully Qualified Survivor* because it hasn't been released yet. When it is, next month, the *NME* will call it 'morbid' and 'Eastern', and very quickly it will be buried and forgotten in its stale jasmine grave until dug up decades later, a pseuds' MacGuffin misinterpreted by the gremlins of hindsight as a lost prophecy of heroic hunkydoriness to come. But it need never have happened and did not need to happen for this moment to arrive.

'. . . and the first thing that the full band will be doing is called "The Width Of Circle".'

The song is so new it's yet to find an ending, and in its unfinished turmoil evaporates in a formless strum to nowhere. But in its looseness, Mick is free to steer where he chooses, David's the pitch, his the markings, swapping squeaky wheels for bending strings and creosote for magnetic fuzz. The opening lines are those of 'Beck's Bolero', paused and stretched, the rest a bumpy semi-automatic boogie. A rough blurry sketch of a grander picture to come.

Polite applause. Peel blesses and bumbles and asks David if he intends to play any gigs with this band. David starts to make a joke, then says yes.

'We're going to do some gigs,' he adds. 'Are we, Michael?'

It is the first time in their 48-hour acquaintance that David has called Mick 'Michael'.

'Michael doesn't really know,' he continues. 'He's just come down from Hull, and I met him for the first time two days ago through John, the drummer, who's worked with me once.'

But Michael does know. By the concert's end, so does the cosmos. The body hears Mick Ronson with the gut first and the ears second, his notes striking the listener from within, vibrating outwards to kiss the skin through vaporous muscle and liquid bone. It is the imprisoned scream of a man who, aged 23, has already spent too many hours with a spade in his hand in the pouring rain suddenly set free in nickel-plated steel, wood and wire.

Mick's refugee mind believes he needs David more than David needs him, unaware of his new friend's ruthless foresight. That, in Mick, David hears the roar of a Kraken waking from ancient, dreamless sleep, and in the power to command it the music of the spheres. His hand already on the leash, he gently tightens the grip.

The concert goes out that Sunday at 4 p.m. when most kids indoors are stomach-rumbling to the final freaky episode of *The Owl Service* before *The Golden Shot*, tea, the weekend bath and *Pick of the Pops*. David tunes in at Haddon Hall before another evening's gig at his Beckenham Arts Lab, where life is still 1969. Two hundred miles away, Mick listens back in Hull where life is still 1949. Peel says his name twice on air in the space of an hour and the city council realise they've just lost a member of their parks department. Smelling a scoop, the local newspaper chases the story to its doorstep. Mick informs them the rumours are true.

'My parents know that this is the only thing I have ever really wanted to do, and I have often felt like banging my head against a brick wall wondering why I wasn't getting anywhere.'

He has been offered jobs in London before, he adds. 'But nothing as secure as this.' The headline spells it out. This is the ex-Rat's 'CHANCE IN BIG TIME'. One week's working notice of creosote and turf is all that stands between him and his new group.

'Formed by pop idol David Bowie.'

THE DAY this news becomes print in a city where tomorrow's chip paper is ever a valuable commodity, the pop idol David Bowie squirms on the lip of a stage under the 14-chandeliered ceiling of the Café Royal's Dubarry Room. He wears a double-breasted caramel corduroy suit and the thinnest of veils over a rictus of unease. His right thigh presses against the left thigh of Cliff Richard, so close that through their fabrics they feel one another's body heat. It is Friday the 13th.

Linking arms the other side of Cliff, who wears a dark jacket, mint-green shirt and tie and thick-rimmed spectacles, is Cilla Black in mini-dress, white go-go boots and the £220 nose she bought herself last birthday. Beside Cilla is wee Lulu, black boots poking from the bottom of a dull brown school ma'am dress. Flanking Lulu are two shaven-headed smiles in orange robes from the Radha Krishna Temple. Beside them is Tony Blackburn in beige suit, pink shirt and blue Crimplene tie. A freak miscellany of colour, couture and character, smashed together for the photographer of *Disc and Music Echo* as poll winners of its Valentine's Day Awards 1970. The Hare Krishnas are friends of George Harrison, there on behalf of the not-quite-yet-officially-dead Beatles to collect their awards for Best Group, LP and Single; Lulu, perplexingly, tops World Girl Singer and, even more so, Best Dressed Girl; Cilla is Top British Girl Singer; Cliff is Best Dressed Male; and David has topped the Brightest Hope category, beating Clodagh Rodgers, Blue Mink, King Crimson, Plastic Ono Band, Karen Young, Humble Pie, Jethro Tull, Creedence Clearwater Revival and Fleetwood Mac. His award is presented by Blackburn, also winner of Top DJ, whose Radio 1 breakfast show is so popular even his imaginary co-hosts Gerald, a chipmunk-voiced pixie, and Arnold, a woofing dog, each receive around a thousand fan letters a week. *Woof! Woof!*

Fun is Blackburn's religion and his congregation has never been bigger; this week he's also been voted Top DJ by readers of rival *Mirabelle*. 'The trouble is that pop music is being taken far too seriously,' chuckles Blackburn. 'People get too involved. It should all be about fun – that's what pop's all about.'

None of this is fun for David. Angie should be here, but it's Ken who has deliberately locked her in the scullery without an invite so he can go to the ball instead. The reward for his skulduggery is a mounted gold seven-inch single in a hinged box – the trophy David collects from Blackburn which is in his hands mere minutes before it's slipped to Ken.

'This is for you,' says David.

A Judas kiss in a leather presentation case, but Ken is too soft-focused by Fleet Street, flock wallpaper, marble, cufflinks, flashbulbs, silver trays and meaningless trinkets to taste its sting. All this is Ken's universe. As pop's Brightest Hope of 1970 it ought to be David's. But he is a trespasser at a show business thanksgiving. An imposter who not a week earlier could be heard on Radio 1 singing about pot and LSD. A not-one-of-them who only last night serenaded the backroom of a pub in Beckenham with his favourite Jacques Brel dirge about the whores of Amsterdam. An illusionist who admits 'I'm very fickle – I'm always changing my mind about things'. An alien who does not know quite who or what he is or where he should be. Only that it is not here in the Café Royal with Tony Blackburn.

Woof! Woof!

EIGHT

HULL: THE SOUND OF IT. Like a leather Bible thumping to the floor. The lonely toll of a sunken ship's bell in its watery grave. Blunt-edged and deadweight.

'And how did the accused murder the victim?'

'Bludgeoned to death by a Hull, m'lud.'

Primordial ugh of simpleton man. The colour of workhouse gruel. Runt sibling disowned by hum and drum. Punchline to its own joke.

'I say, I say, my wife's gone up north.'

'Hull?'

'No, she killed herself of her own accord.'

Hull. The Athens of Nowhere, not even Hull. Yes, Hull. Beautiful, beautiful, *beautiful* Hull!

Drink it in, David! Sup it up, lad! Smell it, suck it, lick the paper and taste it. This is Hull, a real port, not the imagined sailors, fish heads and tails of Belgian chanson but the dockers, ale and grease of Yorkshire living. Glottal-stopped 'ull – a new world, a new universe with new adventures to be had in a new space and time.

The time is the day after he came home to Haddon Hall in his caramel suit without his *Disc* award to pack his bags to drive to Hull. John had instigated the trip when David mentioned that his new car – a Rover to replace his dad's old Fiat – needed servicing. John said he had a mate called Muff Murphy who could do the job cheap. Muff was in Hull. So was Mick, who'd been home a week to sort his affairs and would need ferrying back down again. The obvious plan organised itself. They would all go to Hull – John, David, Angie, Tony and his girlfriend Liz – to service the car, collect Mick and explore what wonders Hull had to offer.

John makes the necessary arrangements, leading the way in his Hillman Minx. First stop, the Turner & Sellers garage in Hessle to drop the Rover into the cheap yet capable hands of Muff Murphy, before David and Angie receive the Brisbane Street hospitality of John's mam and dad. Told to make themselves at home, Angie obliges by ramping up their telephone bill ringing random universities to try and book future gigs. John's dad doesn't mind this so much as David's chosen perch in the living room: sat against the wall half-looking at the television while automatically helping himself to Mr Cambridge's fags. The remaining Haddon Hallers stay with John, eight miles away at his girlfriend's, another Angela, on Arden Road in the market town of Beverley. Tony and Liz are so smitten by its picture-book cobbled streets and Gothic minster they never leave, sparing themselves a glimpse of the unmissable human zoo that is Hull by night. David and Angie, born to safari, will not be similarly denied.

They meet and dine with Mick at The Gainsboro, the city's largest temple to the holy trinity of fat, salt and vinegar. Downstairs for takeaways, upstairs for white cloths on oak tables and waitresses in lace-trimmed aprons with caps like paper boats anchored tight to pinned-back hair. Posh teas with bread and butter on the side and a slice of gateau for afters. The menu an encyclopaedia of North Sea marine life waiting to be given a state funeral of batter and chips on a china plate.

Mick, the local gastronome, orders skate. David, the London boy, plumps for cod. He has no idea what is about to happen.

Neither does Mick, nor Angie; nor will they know even after the moment's passed. Nor will anyone, not even the projectionist across the road in the Cecil cinema who makes it happen. Four months after going on general release, *The Virgin Soldiers* has finally opened in Hull. The film Ken persuaded David to successfully audition for over a year ago. Cast as an extra and forced to chop his hair to a military short back and sides for 40 quid and two seconds on screen. Two seconds of unnoticeable nothing. And yet, now, two improbable seconds of a billion-to-one cosmic coincidence.

David Bowie in the city of Hull, in two places at once. On screen and in chip shop, yards apart on the same stretch of Anlaby Road. The eater and the actor, the physical and the metaphysical, the flesh and the ghost, mutually oblivious to each other's doppelgänged echo location. Fleeting twins of randomly colliding spacetime suspended in semi-sprocket-holed parenthesis.

Until the David in the then of a 1968 Twickenham film set is sucked up into its reel as David in the now of 1970 stabs another chip.

The parallel universes separate. Two seconds gone forever.

DAVID HAS BEEN in the city before but Bowie hasn't. Just over five years ago, Davie Jones & The Manish Boys were bottom of a package bill supporting Gene Pitney at the ABC next to the train station from which John's old group took their name. Another David, another life.

In this name and this life on this day in this place he is scattered in bus shelters, bedroom floors and the cracks of settees in Orchard Park in the pages of this week's *Mirabelle* and *Disc*, respective third Top Male Singer and Number 1 Brightest Hope sharing a split double-page spread with Elvis Presley; it's not mentioned they also share the same birthday.

'I suppose I want success but not for the reason people would think. I want to establish myself so that I can fulfil other desires by using the success as a springboard and then swiftly disestablish myself.'

Hull shrugs and flicks the page with Miners fruit-drop fingernails as outside another phone box smashes.

JOHN REAPPEARS in his Hillman on Sunday as local chauffeur. Angie is happy to stay at home with 'Mr & Mrs Cambo', leaving David to fulfil his other desires at John's chosen rendezvous. The Phoenix Club on Hessle Road is a concrete ark for the working man, describing itself as 'a facility of the highest order to make clubgoing a pleasure'. Sunday's pleasure is usually a girl on stage taking her clothes off and a band on stage keeping theirs on. Only today the upstairs ballroom is closed. No breasts, no beats.

In the packed downstairs lounge bar John orders a pint. Not doing as the Romans do, David asks for a Cherry B.

'Have a pint, you fanny!'

David prefers his bottled poison as it is, sickly sweet but super-strong: half the volume, thrice the dose. He sips and scans the room. Happy ordinary folk in ordinary clothes with ordinary faces hiding ordinary lusts smoking ordinary fags supping ordinary pints swearing ordinary fucking swears having a right ordinary fucking laugh. Imagine.

'Eyes down!'

It is ordinary bingo night. The prize, a few hundred ordinary quid to be won by any of the ordinary folk in any of the ordinary clubs in Hull linked up by the extraordinary fairy godmother of Allied Bingo. The competitor in David cannot resist. There he sits, with his potent thimble of Cherry B, next to John with his pint, in the miasma of smoke and *ee!* and *ay!* and *sorry, lovey* and *bloody 'ell* and legs 11 and doctor's orders gleefully crossing off a sheet of numbers.

Not two miles away on this exquisite Hull evening, the organ pipes above the stage of the City Hall are rattling to the windmills of The Who. Obliviously ordinary on Hessle Road, David Bowie plays bingo.

STRANGER IN A STRANGE LAND, David does not pass through the foreign byways entirely unnoticed. Mick takes him to the café of local ace faces the Gondola – in Hullish, '*gone-dole-uh*' – where twitchy eyes are quick to clock a foreigner in their midst. John takes him to the Jameson Street offices of the *Hull & Yorkshire Times* to guarantee a story in the following Friday's edition. David's official verdict on the city: 'It's OK.' He tells them he enjoyed his tea in The Gainsboro, less so the antique shops along Spring Bank where he and Angie idled fruitlessly through Hullish bric-a-brac. But now that he's two local lads in his new group in the shape of John and Mick, David says he may yet 'make it a second home'.

He spends his last night in the pub with John and their two Angelas. They take the Hillman into the country, to the Railway Inn in Ellerby, 2,000 light years away from anywhere. Narrow winding lanes with signposts directing God knows who to the destinations of Swine and Skirlaugh lead them back into the city. A last pit stop, along from the university on Cottingham Road, in the ultraviolet backroom of the Gardener's Arms.

The pop idol is spotted. A college-girl teenybopper type, the sort he's been talking about in the press as his typical fan. 'Which is odd but nice.' She stares, giggles to her friend, then chooses her moment to approach.

'Ooh! You look just like that David Bowie!'

He takes a nonchalant drag on his cigarette.

'Yeah,' he says with unmistakably unfazed David Bowieness. 'A lot of people tell me that.'

MUFF MURPHY LIVES up to his reputation. David's grey Rover is serviced and ready to be driven back south. So is Mick, collected by David and Angie from Milford Grove, his parents' two-up, two-down council house with a strip of back garden. David feels the familiar panic of Plaistow Grove and recognises he and Mick are survivors of the same terraced claustrophobia. Mick kisses his mother goodbye. She grizzles on the doorstep, watching him wave from the backseat as the car turns one corner then another onto Annandale Road, out of Greatfield, out of Hull, out of sight.

A week passes before a typed letter lands on a doormat in Brisbane Street addressed to 'Mum and Dad Cambo'.

'*Please forgive me for using a typewriter to write this letter to you but David reminded me that it might be a good idea as my writing is so hard to read,*' taps Angie. '*Now before I go any further I want to thank you from David and myself for the most incredible time while we were in Hull. I hope that while we were there you could feel our appreciation instead of this letter being the thing to tell you but I think you know why I have wanted to write and just let you know OFFICIALLY (don't laugh) what marvellous hospitality you possess.*'

It is signed.

'*All our love, see you soon, be careful of that weather in Hull and the sense of humour – I understand it's catching.*'

Intemperate, hilarious Hull. Antiqueless OK promised land of fish'n'chips. Soon to be a London pop idol's second home.

David will return just one more time before he dies.

NINE

THE NAME IS HYPE. His Taste, his Yes, his Egg, his Toast. For now, Hull remains one step ahead of the universe as the only place so far where David's plan to launch a group called Hype has made newsprint. This alone means Hype are doing a very bad job living up to their name.

Hype as an entity exists only in David's head, and even he isn't certain where David Bowie ends and Hype begins. As the readers of the *Hull & Yorkshire Times* alone know, David sees himself and Hype as two separate things. There is David Bowie, the solo artist, and there is David Bowie, the singer with Hype, the group that will make records with and without David Bowie. But the moment David Bowie stops performing as David Bowie and becomes Hype is unclear. Hype, as he's recruited, are himself, Mick on guitar, Tony on bass and John on drums. The music of Hype is the same music as David Bowie plus a few of his favourite cover versions. They've already played one gig for John Peel, but nobody said they were called Hype at the time and it was broadcast by the BBC as plain 'David Bowie'. In David's mind they are definitely Hype when they play their next show at the Roundhouse the Sunday after they return from Hull. But the poster still says 'David Bowie' and though the noise they make knits together as a group, on stage they still look like a singer-songwriter and his three backing musicians. Hype have no understanding of the word.

Hype are David's whim and a prayer to find his place in the 1970s in the pretence of gang leader: not as a pop idol but a pop *group*. They are the reason Mick has left Hull, a pacifier to keep John in his company and another musical project for Tony, who already has his hands full as a jobbing producer. An illusion of fraternity at the mercy of autocracy. The name isn't so much ironic as cynical and the execution clumsy – a sketch of a group that's been ripped too soon from its drawing board, lacking form and colour.

The colour only comes after they've already played seven gigs and the belated advert in *Melody Maker* announcing 'HYPE IS DAVID BOWIE'S NEW ELECTRIC BAND'. It drips from David's hazy conversations about Friedrich Nietzsche and Zarathustra and supermen and Superman into Angie's industry of haberdashery, aided by Liz, to saddle the four horsemen of Hype with their own comic-book costumes.

'Like Dr Strange or the Incredible Hulk.'

Mixing, matching, stitching, sewing, salvaging, scavenging, remodelling, remaking, the pop art alter egos materialise.

David is 'Space Star' in a waist-length cape made of silver netting and blue silk attached to his wrists like batwings. Beneath he wears his favourite zip-up silver jacket, snug underpants worn on top of sparkly silver tights and black knee-length pirate boots.

Tony is 'Hypeman' in stiff-collared vampire green cape and a tight white leotard with a Superman-style 'H' on the chest.

Mick is a more subdued 'Gangsterman', borrowing David's caramel double-breasted suit with black shirt and spotted tie in an effort to look like a rock'n'roll mobster swapping tommy gun for Les Paul.

Which leaves John 'Cowboyman' in a party Stetson which Tony picked out for him from a shop window on Oxford Street, a white shirt frilled with lampshade tassels and his favourite star T-shirt from Kensington Market.

The cartoon is unveiled the second time Hype play the Roundhouse, still billed as 'David Bowie' above the wretched hubbly-bubbling of boiled spew calling itself Genesis. John has arrived ready-cowboyed whereas David, Tony and Mick, still in their Clark Kents, say shazam in the dressing room. To steady the nerves, Mick accepts a puff on some circulated bliss and in a single inhale of regret is teleported to Planet

Mongo. It is a long oblivious journey back for him as Hype kapow and kerplop on stage before a circular shedful of refried hippies.

The shiny costumes do not match the stony music. Hype look light and airy but the sound rumbles from the ground up. The rhythms wallop through Mick's misty-headed electrical storm as David shrieks of mermen, madness and slitting throats. This is not pop music. The only real pop songs Hype have are covers: David's pet talisman, The Velvet Underground's 'I'm Waiting For The Man', Lennon's new single 'Instant Karma!', and another current chart boogie, Canned Heat's 'Let's Work Together'. It is an amateur dramatic pose by a group who have dressed up only to appear dressed up. The fantasy extends no further than the edge of the stage, where, in a plastic Roman centurion's breastplate, eyes fixed on David through a spillage of black ringlets, leans Marc with elbows resting at chin height. A jaguar watching a leopard.

Back in the dressing room, the clothes David, Mick and Tony arrived in have mysteriously vanished. So have Genesis. Space Star, Hypeman and Gangsterman must drive back to Haddon Hall as they are.

The supersuits come out again for their next gig two days later in Sunderland's Locarno Ballroom where heckles of 'poof' keep Wearside safely mired in the 1670s. It is the second and last time Hype ever wear them.

The outfits are never photographed for posterity in the pop papers, nor seen in public again. David's fleeting experiment with panto rock slips between the floorboards of pop history.

Influencing absolutely nothing.

A POP AND ROMANCE MAGAZINE asks David if he has any friends in the entertainment world. He names three.

'Tony Visconti. Marc Bolan. Steve Marriott.'

He tells them he met Marc through Tony, which isn't true – they met years before Tony arrived in London – and that he and Steve have been friends since their 'art school days'.

'I need to be influenced by people, although it would probably be better if I wasn't. I find myself mouthing a few ideas of other people and sometimes I pick up their phrases. The other week I was talking like Marc Bolan but it was quite unintentional.'

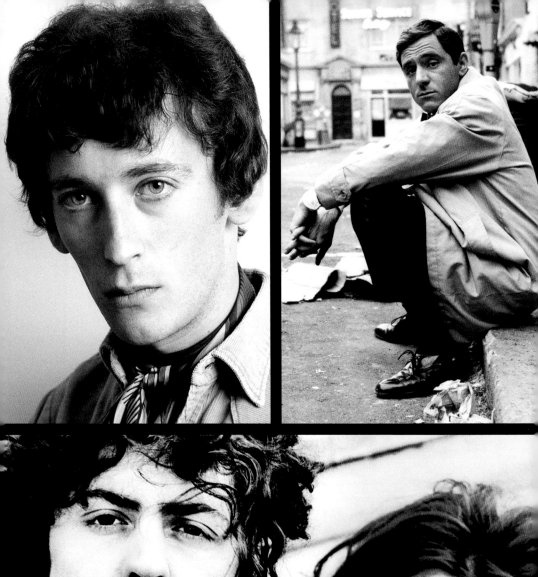

The leopard wants to change its spots to the jaguar.

'A lot of my compositions are very much fantasy tales. I like Marc Bolan's songs very much because he obviously feels the same way.'

In his Blenheim Crescent flat, Marc entertains his own reporter with wine, low-fat cheese and Brussels sprouts to a soundtrack of Johnny Burnette and Frankie Lymon. He talks about Elvis Presley, Vince Taylor and freaking out the kids by going more electric. 'I've always been a fan of early rock'n'roll.'

The jaguar says nothing about the leopard.

THE LEOPARD HAS a new record. It is David's first of the Seventies, 'The Prettiest Star', the one he recorded in early January with the jaguar on guitar. David and Angie decided this song – *her* song – should be the follow-up single to 'Space Oddity' rather than the London song which hasn't even made the B-side. In its place is a leftover from David's last album, 'Conversation Piece', a tune so gentle it's not until the third spin that most listeners realise it's a nervous breakdown in G major.

In the fabric of the universe there is a time and a place for 'The Prettiest Star' but wherever that is, it isn't the British Isles in 1970. Radio waves are untouched by its dim lustre, even if the pop critics are coolly encouraging:

'Not such an original composition as his "Space" hit, but a pleasant performance and quite likely to twinkle at the top of the hit parade.'

. . . and . . .

'This has the most compact catchy melody I've heard. A hit indeed.'

. . . and . . .

'What "Prettiest Star" lacks in the way of a dolly tune, David makes up for by his singing presence. Certainly a hit.'

. . . and . . .

'A sort of country opening, some rambling, scrambling lyric thoughts, but after a couple of plays it falls into place as a melodic and interesting production. CHART CERT!'

'The Prettiest Star' sells fewer than a thousand copies.

★

71

THE UGLY TRUTH about pop. 'It's noisy, it's corny, it's muck. But it gives the masses a lot of joy, happiness and relaxation – and that's the business I'm in.'

As an engineer, Tony Macaulay used to be in the sewage business. As 1970's Mr Pop he's gone from shovelling shit to writing it. At least that's the joke around town, but Macaulay's is the last laugh. Aged 25, he has a million in the bank, a luxury bachelor flat overlooking Hyde Park, a yacht and a Rolls-Royce Silver Phantom with a young female chauffeur in white livery of peaked cap and kinky boots. 'Well, you wouldn't have fellas working for you if you could avoid it, would you?'

For three years now, Macaulay has proved a collaborative King Midas of popular melody. 'Baby, Now That I've Found You' and 'Build Me Up Buttercup' by The Foundations. 'Sorry Suzanne' by The Hollies. 'Let The Heartaches Begin' by Long John Baldry. 'Baby Make It Soon' by Marmalade. 'That Same Old Feeling' by Pickettywitch. And his latest number 1, 'Love Grows' by the group that isn't really Edison Lighthouse. He knocked that one out in 20 minutes flat. Typically he averages a Herculean three songs every fortnight. In terms of their hit parade success rate, he reckons it's around '80 per cent'.

Writing noisy corny muck is a breeze, he says, *if* you know the secret recipe. 'A hit song has got to have two of three ingredients. It's got to have rhythm and it must be catchy or sentimental.' Macaulay's moral: it's not what you shovel but the way that you shovel it.

'I'm giving pop fans what they want. Why be pretentious about it?'

PRETENTIOUS AND UNSENTIMENTAL, David Bowie is still 'A SUPER COOL GUY' in the candy-eyed pages of *Mirabelle*. One who doesn't think he's had many serious relationships.

'In fact I don't think I've had any.'

But he has a lot of girlfriends.

'Some are purely platonic and others are a little more serious.'

He does not mention his fiancée.

'I don't look for anything special in a girl. I mean, if I see a beautiful looking dolly, I won't ask her out just because of her looks.'

Because his brain just doesn't work that way.

'It's personality that appeals to me most. I couldn't care if she had protruding teeth and looked like Dracula, as long as I get on well with her I wouldn't mind!'

Although he's rather moody at times.

'One minute I can be laughing, then the next I will be depressed. But my moods chop and change so much that it's hardly noticeable.'

KEN NOTICES. Ken sees a lot of chopping and changing in David which he likes little and understands less. He only knows that he is losing him: to Angie, to Tony, to invaders from Hull, to the dusk-till-dawn freaks of the Roundhouse, to wishing he was Marc Bolan, roaring wattage and heavy smoke. Ken feels fate's pages turning to an ending like one of the sad children's stories by Oscar Wilde on his Marylebone bookcase, plagued by a foreboding of his being the rose in the gutter.

Suffocating in the Seventies, Ken gasps for air in whichever mirages of yesterday he can find. Tonight, the Royal Albert Hall is such an oasis of old-time blarney courtesy of a charity concert for handicapped children organised by Irish fight promoter Butty Sugrue. The turns include a traditional step-dancing troupe, Johnny Weissmuller's original 'Jane', Hollywood star Maureen O'Sullivan, the popular tenor Josef Locke and Sugrue himself in his capacity as a performing strongman famed for balancing people sat in a chair above his head using only his teeth. What David Bowie is also doing on this bill is a mystery to all but Ken, who has negotiated him a small solo acoustic slot. David is glad only for the chance to meet Locke during the afternoon's rehearsal, shaking hands with the source of the mighty Bogside vibrato never absent from the wireless during his childhood. Voice to voice, David, awed, discreetly collects the older man's autograph.

Outside the Albert Hall, Ken decompresses into 1970 as he and David stroll back to town. Alas, for Ken, they are not alone. Angie is here. These days she is always here, crowding the spaces in David's life Ken most covets: in his confidence, his ear, his music, his home, his bed. Ken fears Angie's fearlessness and is exhausted by her inexhaustible inexhaustibility. There are only so many magazine-award ceremonies he has power enough to bar her from. She will win, Ken knows. But his rose still isn't crushed.

Not until they part company in the Cinzano-lit glow of Piccadilly Circus. Just as David and Angie vanish down the steps to the underground. When David turns to Ken and says, 'Oh, by the way.' Then, with a sheepish smile at Angie, adds, 'We're getting married.'

Ken just stands there, staring at them. And stares. And stares.

He threw the rose into the street, where it fell into the gutter, and a cart-wheel went over it.

TEN

HIS FIRST ALBUM of the Seventies is a gallstone from the Sixties. *The World Of David Bowie*. A different voice, a different haircut, a different pose: Anthony Newley, side-parted mod, the Hans Christian Andersen of Carnaby Street. It's part of Decca's generic *The World Of . . .* series of budget compilations. Mantovani, Val Doonican, Vera Lynn, Jimmy Young. All the greats.

David used to be signed to Decca's imprint Deram, established in 1966 as a home for The Move, Cat Stevens, Amen Corner, The Flower Pot Men and Procol Harum. In between, they released David's first album and three singles. None were hits, but now that David is a *Jackie* mag pop idol they're hoping he has enough new fans prepared to pay the 19 shillings and 11 pence for his old flops. The cover, which he chose, shows a curly David from his recent 'Space Oddity' period wearing the silver zip jacket he still wears in Hype. Only it doesn't fit the tuneful chim-chimmenies within, including a few unreleased leftovers he made with Tony before Decca dropped him. *The World Of David Bowie* is one he no longer inhabits and no one else wants to visit. The *NME* alone faintly praise it as 'pleasantly sung', less impressed by the music than the diction.

'*Though sometimes he puts on a bit of a BBC accent.*'

★

NOT HALF A MILE from the BBC, a telephone rings in Manchester Street. Ken answers and hears the voice of Mrs Jones. It sounds anxious and a little embarrassed. She's heard that her son is going to be married. Ken confirms in grave tones that this is what David has told him.

Married?

Yes.

To Angie?

Afraid so.

Ken knows in Mrs Jones – 'Peggy' to her friends – he has an ally against a common enemy both have mentally pigeonholed as the Great Whore of Babylon, Mother of Harlots and Abominations of the Earth. She, like him, has been excluded from any arrangements. Ken sympathises but is unable to supply her with any more information. Peggy thanks him and hangs up.

The telephone rings again in Manchester Street. Ken answers. Peggy again, now urgent and excitable. She has *news*!

A time!

'Tomorrow at 11.'

And a place!

'Bromley Register Office.'

She asks Ken if he'll attend. He tells her no. Not unless David calls to invite him, which he doesn't suspect will happen. He suspects right.

That night on Southend Road, David slips and slides in seven seas of warm female.

In Manchester Street, Ken says goodnight to Bobby the bear and turns out the light.

HER NAME IS CLARE. She is 21, an uninspired model and aspiring artist. Theda Bara from the neck up, Twiggy from the neck down. Hers are the startled panda eyes, delicate limbs and fag-end nipples on the British poster for Andy Warhol's *Chelsea Girls* where her then-teenage naked body substituted for the bricks and mortar of New York's Chelsea Hotel; its designer was later threatened with arrest under pornography offences. David has known Clare for almost a year, as a friend and occasional bosom to cry on in the ebb and flow between Hermione and Angie and all shores in between. She is gorgeous, Angie agrees, and on the eve of their wedding, she is theirs and they are hers.

They'd spent that afternoon buying some last ceremonial rags from the triple-tiered moochers' paradise that is Kensington Market, a labyrinthine bazaar of lock-ups selling everything and anything that flops, flounces, dangles and jangles, where Angie bought a long pink and purple floral print dress and David a pair of charisma-hugging black satin trousers. These are the clothes that lie hanging around them as they wake, all three, shagged and fagged, the bride, the groom and their witness, blinking the grit of bliss from their eyes as consciousness slowly jigsaws their memories back together.

Late Thursday . . . the back of The Three Tuns . . . a new folk night run by their friends Ian and Ken . . . David, solo, singing his 'Wild Eyed Boy From Freecloud' . . . coming home with Clare . . . unholy trinities . . . unselfish pleasures . . . the golden voyage on the seven seas . . .

The . . .

      night . . .

           before . . .

THE PLAY WITHIN the play is ready to begin. Other than the principal actors in the roles of bride and groom, the cast is threadbare. Conspicuous absentees from today's performance are many. There is no Tony, who couldn't take the day off production work. There is no Mick, who has gone back to Hull for the weekend. Less surprisingly, there is no Marc, and no Steve Marriott, his other 'best friend' from the entertainment world. There is no Ken, of course, and no Lindsay who cannot be trusted not to interrupt any 'I do's with a quick slit of the wrist. There is no Mary from the Arts Lab and none of David's old school friends. And there is nobody from The Cane.

In their place are the remaining vagabonds of Haddon Hall – John, Liz with the surname like a jam, Roger the Lodger and the occasional Nita – along with their overnight guest Clare.

Peggy is also here, hatted and stiffly top-buttoned in matching jacket and skirt. As an added surprise for the bride and groom, she's taken the liberty of inviting members of the local press to document the wedding of her pop idol son; they're already milling on the pavement on London Road with pencils sharpened and cameras loaded.

Overslept but not overdressed, the groom augments his new Kenny Market trousers with a flowery shirt, necktie and *that* super-white Afghan coat. The bride complements her floral dress with a scarf and pink shoes.

Everyone in their place, the performance begins.

BROMLEY REGISTER OFFICE PRESENTS

The Wedding of
David Robert Jones
&
Mary Angela Barnett

A comedy, pursuant to the Marriage Act of 1949.

Curtain up. Act One of one.

The witnesses seated, the bride and groom stand with the plump registrar who proceeds to gobble and gook about solemn declarations, and lawful impediments, and persons present, and duly sanctioning, and entering voluntarily, and commitment and binding and care and support and faith and loyalty and love and happiness. They are legal words and formal words and some of them are beautiful words. But they are all just words which burst upon the eardrums of the bride and groom like so many pretty soap bubbles. David and Angie nod their heads and exchange knowing smiles, according to their parts as scripted.

'With this ring . . .'

The rings are rings, but not finger rings – rings for the wrist. Four silver bangles from Peru, a gift from Angie's older brother. Shared two apiece, they slip on easily and will slip off just as quickly, but they are ringly enough for legal purposes, even if Peggy cannot help twitch her tight lips with shrewish unease as they gaily jingle at the moment of matrimony.

The drama reaching its conclusion, bride and groom kiss, hands clap and the official certificate is presented for signature.

David Robert Jones, a 23-year-old bachelor musician of Flat 7, 42 Southend Road, Beckenham, son of publicity officer Haywood Stenton Jones (deceased).

Mary Angela Barnett, a 20-year-old spinster student of Flat 7, 42 Southend Road, Beckenham, daughter of mining engineer George Milton Barnett.

David's autograph is big, disjointed with spiky capitals. Angie's bigger, smoother, with flowing loops and a decisive crossed double T. Best man and nominated witness John stands close, preparing to take the pen next. Before he can, another hand thrusts in and seizes it. Peggy's grip is firm. David can do nothing to stop her leaning forward to sign the book in John's place. Hers is a small, tight 'M. M. Jones' for Mary Margaret. The pen is passed to the second witness, 'Clare Noel Shenstone'. And the deed is done. By common law, David and Angie are now Mr & Mrs Jones.

Close curtains and applause.

THERE IS NO CONFETTI, only a few photographs of the bride, groom and mother-in-law for the men from the papers, who follow their trail across the road to The Swan And Mitre where their guests toast their happiness and David gives his first interview as a married man. He tells them that he has no honeymoon plans.

'Unfortunately, I'm far too busy working.'

They remain in the pub that lunchtime before the party disbands and the nobles of Haddon Hall drive home to as normal a Friday evening as its mischievous spirits ever allow. David will remember nothing about his wedding night, only that he spends it there, with his wife, and his friends, watching the television like courtiers after a banquet, aching for masques and revels to ease the anguish of a torturing hour between aftersupper and bedtime.

So how might they and their countrymen beguile the lazy time this 79th day of the Seventies?

MOST TRANSPORT FOR mirth to Oil Drum Lane in the province of Shepherd's Bush. Residence to a reseller of refuse named Albert and his son, Harold, who this week has befriended a wealthy antiques dealer of suspiciously delicate manners.

'He's a poof!' deduces Albert. 'He's as bent as a boomerang!'

Harold withers. 'I don't understand you. You've got it on the brain. You've got poofmania! Everybody on television is a poof! The announcers, the newsreaders, even the weathermen – they're all poofs!'

Ignoring his father's wise warnings, Harold cultivates his friendship with the dealer, accepting small trinkets of affection including tickets to the ballet.

Albert despairs. 'Poofs' football!'

Until the fait accompli, a private dinner for two at the antique dealer's apartment, *homo et homo*. A pass is made and Harold recoils. Fleeing the scene in shame, he suddenly remembers his father's earlier appeal to stick 'to the straight and narrow' by calling on local bird Dolly Miller and giving her 'a seeing to'. Craving salvation, Harold does precisely that.

Albert is at first relieved, then disgusted. 'You dirty little devil!'

Whereupon studio applause and the jovial knock-kneed melody of Mr Grainer and his 'Old Ned' signals the end of these inoffensive festivities, typically tickling the bellies of 20 million. Blessed Britannia of iron hoofs, pansies, poofs and queer-bashers – laugh long and laugh hard!

ELEVEN

MORNING BREAKS ON a new era in Haddon Hall. Yesterday it was the bohemian Xanadu of David and Angie and their friends. Today it is the Camelot of Lord and Lady Bowie and their chosen attendants. The transformation is immediate.

With marriage comes money – a cheque for a thousand dollars sent from Col Barnett, Angie's father in Cyprus – and with money comes materialism. Lady Bowie invests her dowry in furnishing their palace and educating her lord on the art of interior design. Angie introduces his fingertips to the tactile delights of London's dockside warehouses where her Persian-rugged Cypriot upbringing is put to use selecting exotic utilitarian carpets to cover Haddon Hall's bare wooden floors. Closer to home, The Stable Door antique shop and auction house off Beckenham High Street lures them with a monstrous marble-topped Burmese sideboard adorned with dragons which they repaint white. It is accompanied by a French hand-carved four-poster bed, bought in pieces which they assemble with the zeal of two cats building a bird table. New colour is introduced in the living room, repainted an aristocratic dark olive green, and the curtains dyed a juicy red. And everywhere, every day, or so it seems to those under the same moulded ceilings, another new objet d'art appears. A peacock-tail fan. Tiffany glassware. Chinese silk. A Japanese desk. A Gamet art deco vase.

Piece by piece, they are constructing a stage set for a drama yet to be written. They make it together, but it is Angie who intuitively directs the action. Hers are the eyes of a Hollywood soundstage and David its star talent. She alone knows best how to light him and what angles to shoot from: create for him this world in private so that he can go forth and conquer the one beyond in public. This is her plan. Invent from the inside, from the bare floorboards up. Prepare, scheme and dress-rehearse then activate, execute and win. Cocoon in fantasy, then emerge and make an epic of reality.

But the daily pace of Haddon Hall can't wholly surrender to fantasy just yet. There is still food to be bought and bills to be paid. There is still laundry to do in the twin-tub washing machine and spin dryer, both on tick from the London Electricity Board, their rattling metal carbuncles spoiling the antiquity of the hallway. And there are still five other bodies sharing their oxygen. For now.

SATURDAY IN SOHO. Its cross streets bustling with weekenders, out-of-towners, in-crowders and knocking-shoppers seeking beer or espresso or dim lights or loud music or fab gear or foreign food or mucky pictures or cheap flesh or whatever else it is they imagine they'll find here if they lurk and gawp long enough at the neon, the windows, the girls, the boys, the beaded doorways and the pandemonium of XXXs. The scent of urgency, of a thousand cigarettes half-smoked in haste, of fast-frying meat, of heavy perfumes and lacquers buzzing in one giant swarm of man bait, of the exhaust fumes of beeping cars, of steamed milk and spilt ale and hot sugar. And, weaving in the gaps between, hand in hand, step the newly-wed Mr & Mrs Jones.

Tony is waiting for them at Trident with the rest of Hype. It is David's first studio session since forming his new band, though the song they're here to record is an old one from his previous album – 'Memory Of A Free Festival'. The original was an eight-minute celebration of an event he and his Arts Lab friends organised last summer in Beckenham. The song's first half is a Dylanish meander like an even paler 'Whiter Shade Of Pale'. The second is a not-pale-enough 'Hey Jude', replacing all the *na-nas* with a hand-holding salutation to a spaceship – the bit Marc and

June had been dragged into last September as part of its spontaneous studio choir with the occasional Nita from Haddon Hall and anyone else with a willing pair of lungs who happened to be passing.

Six months on, Tony's persuaded David he should remake it with a new arrangement as his next single, adamant that he can somehow chop and condense it into a radio-friendly hit. After the collapse of 'The Prettiest Star', David needs one.

The single takes several days to complete. David drafts in the emergency services of his former Philips A&R man Ralph Mace, a classically trained concert pianist who helps add a part written for Moog synthesizer. Tony's new arrangement is full colour and full contrast. When it's finished, David's hippie hymn to a summer's day of communal enlightenment has been frazzled by the bright lights of Broadway. It now sounds like overstated rock opera, a showstopper from *Hair* letting in the same sunshine. Carried away in its new theatricality, David sings with gurning affectation, twisting paint as '*pint*', brain as '*brine*' and away as '*a why*'. But the saving grace is its whipcords of northern light. The first record by David Bowie to feature Mick Ronson detonates him like a warhead. His licks are precision blasts: short, simple, melodic, piercing, vibrating their last phrases in radiation clouds of full gain sustain. He pulls out his every Jeff Beckism, flicking his pick-up selector in hiccups of hot feedback, low twanging and high squealing, the helium core of David's hallelujah to the sun machine.

There is time enough to spare in Trident to toy with one of David's new songs, an eerie brontosaurus stomp about gods and Nietzschean master races called 'The Supermen'. The tune is simple, the tricky words made trickier by David's epidemic vowel contortions about '*strynge gimes*', the rhythm a paradiddle too far for John. Just one little section, but he strains to lock into the required groove. It's not David nor Tony but Mick who snaps.

'Come on! It's fucking easy!'

John is unprepared for this Humber wrath. Not from Mick. Not his *mate*. The vibe is killed and the air turned to Kryptonite. Tony suggests they all take a break and John is the first one outside for some air. David and Angie follow and suggest they all share a spirit-raiser round the corner in La Chasse. It's the usual half-pissed post-midnight post-Marquee musician crowd. Wannabes, gonnabes, couldabeens and neverbeens.

The only face John recognises is one of Ashton, Gardner & Dyke, though which of the three he can never remember. They're bleary-eyed, pint in hand, prodding a cackling joke-shop laughing bag when they turn and see David. 'I'm sick o' this bastard,' they say, giving it another flick. 'Getting on me fucking nerves all night!' Their cue to fast-bowl it across the bar. The bag smacks against the far wall, dropping to the floor with another demented chortle.

'AHAWHAHAHEEHAHAAA!'

It's all the balm John needs. One pint and he's laughing loud as the bag. David reassures him everything will be OK. Drinks drained, they return to find the studio tension diffused. But it's only because he's not looking for it that John doesn't see in Mick's eyes the shrapnel of the conversation held with Tony in his absence. A glisten of guilty sadness that wasn't there an hour ago.

THE NEXT DAY, a different studio. London Weekend Television is a stray penalty kick north of Wembley Stadium, national laugh factory of *On the Buses* and *Please Sir!* Not so far from the set of Fenn Street Secondary Modern, deep in its concrete guts is a small recording facility, primarily for TV themes and jingles. Tony was here last week, messing around with his own solo project, Yankee Dayglo, and their obscurity-doomed 'Dee Dah Shuka Shuka Doo Dah'. Today he's back with John and their old session friend Rick Wakeman to concoct further pop mischief with Marc. Mick has come too, purely to observe, a scholar in the shadows paying close attention to Tony's hands on the mixing desk. The alert apprentice asks questions, but not so many to arouse suspicions that he may be more than an intrigued yokel from the North.

Last night in Trident was hard labour. Today is easy play. There is no David and so none of his frowning chords and brown leathery verses smelling of heady books and overthinking. The air here is pink and yellow like the tune Marc has brought, a gambolling groove trained to the hips. The words are rock'n'roll powder puff. Marc doesn't need Nietzsche when he's got Dale Hawkins. *'Baby, baby!'* It's that simple.

The song is something Marc bounced around with Tony while they were making the new Tyrannosaurus Rex album *A Beard Of Stars*. He never finished it because he knew that the sketchy 'Oh Baby' didn't fit with the usual Tyrannosaurus Rex bops about Avalon, sun lieges and silver satyrs. This was basic, repetitious dance-floor lust: pop as iced cola and catchy as nits.

It was Tony, ever the bright ideas man, who suggested they throw a bunch of musicians at Marc's demo and try to put it out under a secret pseudonym. To help mask Marc's vocals, Tony himself will sing lead. Together, they, John and Rick will be the made-up band. No point trying to fool anyone. The crazier the better. Something far out and otherworldly that still sounded rock'n'roll, but strung out from another dimension. A name that sounds like insects from outer space.

Dib Cochran & The Earwigs.

'Oh, baby! Ooh!'

Wocca-wocca-wocca-wocca!

'Oh, baby!'

Oh, baby, baby! What Dan Dare doo-wop. What space-age jukebox jive. What glorious bastard of pop's past and style's future. What twinkling concentrate needing only speaker, glitter and teenager to shake up and explode in a plastic infinity of diamond star halos, automatic shoes, sabre-tooth dreams, fleet-foot voodoo, alligator rain, hot love and easy action. What angel of the lord of youth. What *sound.*

What sound?

This sound, the sound of Marc following hepcat visionary instinct, unaware where he's going, the sound of disco and strings and dance and rock soda jerked into one, the sound of nothing else like it at this point in pop, the sound of an experimental joke that has far more serious implications for the future of humankind than any of its participants can possibly comprehend. The sound of 'Oh Baby' by Dib Cochran & The Earwigs is the sound of the Seventies newborn. Just waiting for the right name. The right look. The right hype.

IT'S ALL A BLOODY HYPE. The band know it, the organisers know it, the plane of 133 journalists and photographers flying from London to New York to see it know it, and so will everyone who ever reads about it when it becomes inky comic relief between mailbag moans about

The Beatles splitting up and ads for 'Rape' by Peter Wyngarde. But there are madmen with the money to blow, the nerve to do it and the dream to believe it might actually work. The scam: to launch a band from Tunbridge Wells just signed to United Artists by booking them a gig supporting Van Morrison in glamorous New York. The plan: chartering a plane to be filled with invited representatives of every British music publication going, lured by the irresistible offer of a free round trip to America, watered and fed there and back, a chauffeured limo to the Royal Manhattan Hotel and a front-row seat at the gig itself. The hype: witnessing said journalists' payola pearls of pristine copy in next week's papers transforming a bunch of nobodies into an overnight sensation. The price of fame: a £30,000 freeloaders' jolly.

The hypers are called Famepushers, a new management company who might know how to push fame but not an Aer Lingus Boeing 707 off a runway on time. The journalists' 10 a.m. take-off becomes a 2 p.m. take-off, delayed by an emergency stop in Ireland to fix the brakes before a 6 p.m. take-off. By then only the pilot is sober enough to care and the press have stopped trying to work out what Olga Deterding is doing on board. The eccentric oil heiress, wrists still scarred from slashing them the night she broke up with Alan Whicker, sits with her new beau from *Candid Camera*, his son and the groupie who wrote *Groupie*. The Irish stewardesses keep on pouring and the smoke turns ever more Persian.

The scheduled lunchtime arrival into JFK becomes a Saturday night arrival as the pre-booked motorcade of 26 Cadillacs flanked by police escort hit rush-hour traffic. Racing against the clock, the chauffeurs are told to forego the hotel and head straight to the venue. Only a portion make it through the gridlock on time to the Fillmore East. This, the end of the rainbow, a scuzzy converted cinema on the Lower East Side where the half-alive are dragged out of their limos and into their seats. More drinks are poured and wacky smoke billows.

The group nobody has ever heard of but who everyone has been flown 2,200 miles to fall in love with finally walk on stage. A few poppy flop singles ago they were called Kippington Lodge. A terrible name, so their guitarist, an Anglo-German named Brinsley Schwarz, decided to change it. Unfortunately for them he changed it to his name, Brinsley Schwarz. Whatever that conjures – a standard issue Wehrmacht pistol, a Bavarian delicacy of pickled horse – it isn't four blokes from Tunbridge Wells trying to sound like The Band. Their first song on stage at the Fillmore East lasts 12 minutes. The journalists sit and stare and numbly smile with jet-lagged eyes that threaten to cry neat Scotch. They have now been awake over 20 hours.

Once safely back in London, the transatlantic hangovers pass sobering judgement. Brinsley Schwarz are found guilty of perpetrating 'the biggest hype of all time' and Famepushers pick up a £30,000 bill for overnight infamy. Neither their debut single nor debut album makes the Top 40. Nothing they ever release ever will. Just as Beanz Meanz Heinz, Brinsley Schwarz meanz hype. And in the music wars of 1970, hype has just become a very dirty word.

HYPE'S DRUMMER SEES more dangers but doesn't realise he's seen them until the knife is embedded between his shoulder blades. Only then will John replay the scenes in his mind, piecing together his sudden fate in gorily slow motion.

Maybe it was the jokes. Not everybody could handle John's jokes but that's just the way he was. Spies a gap in conversation no thicker than a fag paper and he'll plug it with a wad of daft.

'Tobacco. Who found tobacco, David? That's right. Sir Walter Raleigh. And what else did he find? Potatoes. Imagine, David, if he'd gorr 'em mixed up? We'd all be sitting round trying to light King Edwards!'

No. It couldn't have been *just* the jokes. Maybe he was too friendly? David liked John. Always did. No side to John. Never wanted anything from David other than play in his band and be his mate, go for a pint and have a laugh and a game of darts or a kick around in the garden. Maybe David liked him to a weakness. Needs to screw his courage to the sticking place, thinks Lady Bowie. Takes a ruthless plough to harvest success. No time for friends when you're thane of Haddon Hall that shall be King hereafter.

It all starts to add up. That day Benny was here. Mick invited their old singer from The Rats to stay a few nights in Haddon Hall. Purely social, John thought, until he left them to grab some shopping in his car and came back to find Benny with Mick and Tony listening to a demo acetate of The Rats. Not the line-up John played in but the later line-up with a new drummer. Another Mick – 'Pecker', as John and others knew him back in Hull. Or 'Woody' as he preferred in a town of too many Micks, short for his surname, like the local village: Woodmansey. John was told Tony wanted to hear The Rats to help Benny get them a deal. That should have rung his skull like an alarm bell there and then. But it didn't. And so it comes.

It comes under a silver cloud. A small one that John's trying to make bigger but the bloody gizmo in his hand won't work. The silver cloud is supposed to smother David and Angie's bedroom ceiling. John is helping to paint it for them, but it's tricky work because of the repeated moulding design. To make it easier, he's picked up a special spray gun from a DIY shop, a glass bottle with a long nozzle. But the paint is too thick and the nozzle is clogged. The silver cloud is only a silver splodge and John is forced to do it the long and fiddly way, using a brush and balancing on a stepladder on an early April afternoon.

The bedroom windows have been opened to ventilate the paint fumes. It means when David and Angie return in their Rover and park at the side of the house, John can hear everything. The pebbles crunching in the drive. The engine coughing to a stop. The passenger door opening.

Angie's voice, clear and commanding. 'You've *got* to tell him!'

John stops dabbing the ceiling.

So, then. Here it comes.

The shake of the front door. Footsteps, voices. A hinge creaks.

'John? Can I have a word?'

The word is wrapped in cotton wool because David knows no other way to deliver it. The word is many words but to John's ears it all blurs into one. *'The–thing–is–John–we've–been–talking–and–we've–decided–that– we're–going–to–get–another–drummer–for–the–group–so–now–I–want–you–to– know–one–thing–and–it's–very–important–you–know–it–but–it's–not–you– John–it–really–isn't–it's–just–that–what–we–really–need–is–a–drummer–who– can–also–help–with–the–musical–arrangements–and–that's–the–only–reason– and–the–other–thing–I–want–you–to–know–and–it's–very–important–you– know–it–is–that–you–don't–have–to–leave–you–can–stay–here–with–us–and– none–of–this–is–about–you–John–because–I–want–you–to–know–one–thing– and–it's–very–important–you–know–it . . .'*

John hears the word for what it is. So that's the reasoning. They want a musical arranger. An ideas man. Like the idea of how to bridge the two halves of the new 'Memory Of A Free Festival' by bashing a cymbal with a mallet then playing it backwards so the sound sucks up to a dramatic halt. Which was John's idea. But, still. They want a musical arranger.

Mick says nothing to John. Nor does Tony. It is a Monday evening. *The High Chaparral. Up Pompeii! Doomwatch.* John's in no mood for any of it.

The next morning he rises with the dawn and loads his drums into the back of his Hillman. *Tambourine ka-bash! Smash! Smash! Tambourine ka-bash!* It's a noisy business. On the other mattresses the conspicuously motionless slug-like shapes of Mick and Roger don't flinch. Nobody comes out of the other bedrooms to wave him off. John doesn't linger. The gear in, he slams the driver's door, turns the ignition and shoos Haddon Hall from his rear-view mirror without a second glance.

He takes with him a maraca of David's he'd forgotten was kept in his kit box, his Hype cowboy hat and the five-pound note he borrowed the night before. John told David he needed it for petrol but uses only two pounds on fuel. The rest he spends at a post office in Kensington, putting his faith in ERNIE by investing in Premium Bonds. He can see his dad, fag in mouth, paper in hand, checking the winning numbers every month. 'Kent! The winners are always in bloody Kent!' John, on his way home from Kent, hopes he might be in luck. The cashier rubber stamps his bonds.

B O W 8.

And the gods laugh.

The lime-and-cream Hillman weaves out of West London following signs for the North. John is home in Hull long before the fryers are hot and smoking for teatime.

TWELVE

PECKER IS IN. He is in before John is out. While John is painting David's ceiling, Woody has already had the phone call, and a new contract for Hype has been drawn up in preparation for his signature. At first, Woody isn't sure: about David, about moving south, about leaving his secure job at a spectacles factory in Palookaville, East Yorkshire. But Mick convinces him he has nothing to lose.

'You're gonna do fuck all up in Hull.'

It's true. Woody has just turned 20. Palookaville is Driffield, two dozen country miles north of the celestial city of Hull and 15 inland from the penny arcades of Bridlington: the best thing anyone can say about Driffield is that it isn't its next-door neighbour, Nafferton.

Mick first spotted Woody paying kit service to the Stones and John Mayall's Bluesbreakers in local yokels The Roadrunners. Pecker's beat was mean, his sticks lightning rods of vented rage: at being turfed out of school labelled a useless class clown; at his violent ex-army father's domestic blitzkriegs of crockery smashing; at the certainty of the rest of his life in Palookaville, East Yorkshire.

Woody has been a Rat not 12 months. He was Mick's first choice when John left in April '69, hired as their replacement drummer on the shop floor of the Vertex spectacles factory where Mick and the remaining band found him working overtime one Sunday after driving to Driffield specifically to press-gang him into service. He didn't resist. The Rats' heavy machinery, oiled with Hendrix, Mayall, Beck and Cream, was the rock'n'roll industry Woody liked best. That winter they recorded two tracks of hot denim stink at the same home studio where 'Bernie Gripplestone' rose and fell – one a honky original, the other a cover of Mayall's 'Telephone Blues'. This was the demo Mick played Tony in Haddon Hall. Without being there in person, Woody passed the audition.

It takes a weekend of deliberation and a two-pronged telephone attack from David, then Mick, before Woody accepts. He lets David know on the Monday morning. On the Monday afternoon David has his pep talk with John. John is gone by the Tuesday lunchtime and by the weekend there's a new body on John's old mattress in Haddon Hall.

Woody is quieter, hairier, smokier and a little drier of humour than John, though his accent rattles the windowpanes with the same soft Hullish drone. David listens, absorbs, mimics. '*Ur nur, av gorra gur up rurd on me urn.*' Young, overly keen and a little heavy-handed, he has only just got his bearings in Haddon Hall when he slips with a kitchen knife, slicing his finger to the bone. Woody has three stitches and Hype suddenly have a drummer who cannot drum until the wound heals. There is nothing they can do.

THE CIRCUIT'S DEAD. There's something wrong.

'*Houston, we've got a problem here.*'

Two days after three astronauts leave earth bound for the moon, an oxygen tank explodes, damaging their craft, sabotaging their mission and placing their fate in the hands of mathematics, luck and the combined prayers of a world white-knuckling with worry from Midnight Mass in Westminster to the Wailing Wall. A human tragedy unimaginable beyond the words of a recent popular song none of the papers dare mention. The daily headlines write their own verse.

Wednesday: shock.

THE WORLD IS PRAYING

THE HOURS OF HOPE

GOOD LUCK, APOLLO 13!

Thursday: desperation.

THE PERILOUS HOURS

THE GRIM BATTLE

I A.M. POWER FAILURE IN APOLLO 13

Friday: courage.

THEY'LL BE HOME AT SEVEN

THE WORLD WAITS

APOLLO CAN MAKE IT!

Saturday: salvation.

AMEN!

BEAUTIFUL!

THANK GOD!

The three astronauts were saved by science but all dues are given to heaven. After splashdown in the South Pacific they're flown to a naval recovery ship, welcomed by salutes and a military band. The first music they hear back on earth is by Richard Strauss.

The theme from *2001: A Space Odyssey*.

LAURENCE MYERS NEVER wanted to be an accountant. He is too charming a North London Jewish boy for a fate of ledgers and double-entry systems, and by his own admission not very good at it. He jokes that if he were a doctor he'd be done for killing people. As an accountant he's got away with murder long enough to make a career of it. But he wants out, and, making a clean slate of 1970, he gets out.

He's spent the last few years in practice bean-counting for the entertainment industry, handling accounts for producer Mickie Most and working with the Rolling Stones. Laurence loves the smell of the greasepaint far more than he does the whiff of carbon paper and slowly turns his thoughts towards artist management. His first client is Mike Leander, an established producer, arranger and writer for Billy Fury, Marianne Faithfull and Paul Jones, who's currently trying to find the breakthrough vehicle for his old friend, an umpteen-times-flop rocker born Paul Gadd but currently calling himself Paul Raven. His second is pop's King Midas of muck, Tony Macaulay, number 1 drain-blocker of Edison Lighthouse's 'Love Grows', which Laurence personally negotiated in a deal with Bell Records. It's the Bell money which finally allows Laurence to retire from accountancy at the age of 33 and launch his own management company. He names it Gem.

Gem set up offices in the heart of town, Regent Arcade House just off Oxford Circus, in what was once a showroom for Warner's corsets and bras. Three floors up from the thunder of footfall and the number 12 to Croydon, where eyes once popped over Sta-Up-Top girdles and hands shaken over the strapless wonder of the Good News, Laurence envisions his very own Brill Building – an equivalent hive of offices for worker-bee writers and producers buzzing ideas for the next number 1, where pluggers, journalists, managers and artists will swap numbers and scurrilous gossip, and where tomorrow's stars are born today.

The showroom needs little conversion. Laurence slices it up into a conference room, a reception area and a series of small offices: one for himself, one for Tony Macaulay and his all-female team, another for Macaulay's gorgeous plugger and ex-girlfriend Anya Wilson, another for Mike Leander and his ubiquitous loose end of an office boy Paul Raven, leaving the rest spare for others to join them.

Word spreading and love growing, Gem's phone starts to ring.

'Laurence? It's Tony Defries.'

Tony Defries. Lawyer with Godfrey, Davis & Batt. Before that Martin Boston & Co. Even though he isn't a qualified solicitor, nor does he look like one. Defries is a legal clerk with a nose like a bomb and hair like its explosion who dresses in a strange Victorian frock coat, a stray Dickensian apparition belonging to an 800-page novel all the duller for his absence. That's how he first walked into Laurence's life back in the Sixties: he, the accountant, Defries, the legal muscle hired to help Mickie Most – or rather his manager Allen Klein – fight a lawsuit. Klein was already burying bodies for the Rolling Stones and would soon do the same for The Beatles. He had a reputation in Sixties pop similar to that of Al Capone in Twenties Chicago. Klein liked it that way. He didn't need friends, nor did he want them. He wanted money, power and the gonads of every record company's managing director swinging on his desk in a Newton's cradle. He got them, too. He was a pomade-slicked, pipe-sucking mobster in a world of tea-pouring sirs and trimmed moustaches who reacted to his business methods as they might to a man with a baseball bat arriving for a game of tiddlywinks. He was loathed by more than he was loved, but to those who loved him the greatest thing about Allen Klein was that he did not give a supersonic fuck about the opinion of anybody in the entire universe other than himself. And nobody loved Klein more than Tony Defries.

After winning the Most/Klein case, Laurence and Defries kept in touch, sometimes dining on the pretence of business for tax-deductible pleasure under the plastic grapes of 'the Tratt' – Soho's in-crowdiest eatery, La Trattoria Terrazza, where Mick Jagger and Michael Caine could often be found sucking on sautéed calf's kidneys. He and Defries were there only the other month, lunching with a delegation of London's top fashion models who wanted help negotiating better contracts, their table at the Tratt like *The Last Supper* by *Cosmopolitan*. In fact, he hasn't heard from Defries since. Until now.

'Tony! What can I do for you?'

A slow careful voice purrs down the receiver.

'Laurence? I've been consulted by David Bowie. Do you know who he is?'

THE LETTER SLIPS from Ken's hands. He'd read it standing up but sits down to digest.

So. The End.

He removes his glasses, gives them a nervous wipe, replaces them with a poke on the bridge of his nose then picks the letter up from the floor to read again. It is from David. It has his address and his signature but none of his soul. The words are not David-type words. They're machine words, pieces of legal Meccano slotted together cog to cog, a syntax mathematical formula spelling only pain, cost and sadness.

$$(\textit{I have been advised})^{db} = \sum_{\textit{past endeavours}}^{\textit{our agreement}} \left(\frac{k}{p} \right) \textit{career thereunder}$$

But there's the cold ugly truth.

I have been advised.

The characters rearrange themselves through Ken's lenses.

You have been betrayed. I don't need you any more. Others have taken your place to pull my strings and this is their first sharp tug. You are no longer my manager and I am no longer your client. We are finished.

It tolls the death of Ken's personal *Pygmalion*: the portfolio artiste he's spent years sculpting from a teenage mod neophyte into a songwriter, musician, theatre professional and screen actor. The boy he himself turned from Jones to Bowie. Professor Pitt still had big plans for his Eliza. Treading the boards at the Harrogate Festival, performing some 'mime' and singing in broad Scots as musical narrator of a theatrical adaptation of Sir Walter Scott's *The Fair Maid of Perth*. Curtain calls, bows, applause and bouquets. This was Ken's vision for David Bowie in 1970. He'd written a plan-of-action list with seven similar objectives for the year ahead; at the very bottom, the prospect of David having another hit record.

On the paintwork by the telephone in Haddon Hall David has scrawled his own objective.

'Not conformity but radical.'

Above the word conformity he adds two words: 'Ken Pitt.'

The literal writing on the wall.

KEN PLACES THE LETTER ASIDE, eyes focusing on an unfocused nothingness of empty space. The space where David had sat three weeks ago when he'd last visited Manchester Street. The omens were all there then, twitching in the muscles of David's gloom-struck frown like the lurid cover of a cheap paperback thriller: *The Terrible Murder of Kenneth Pitt*. He'd been like a child sulking only to stop from crying.

He even said it out loud. 'I want to have a go at managing myself.'

The dagger was drawn. Ken did not believe he'd actually have the nerve to plunge it. David didn't. Not that day, at least, dissuaded by a placating cheque for £200 which Ken had given as an advance and which David had received as due ransom. But now, this.

I have been advised.

Ken is sure he knows whodunit. *The Terrible Murder of Kenneth Pitt* was committed by Angie. David's kicker of doors and grabber of lapels; the screech that silences the room so David can be heard; the bark on the other end of the phone that never hangs up until no becomes yes; his boardroom Boadicea willing to trample anyone and anything standing between her man and his due success. Angie, David's adviser. Angie, Ken's despatcher.

But Ken is only half right. The plot is more complicated than he can possibly imagine and Angie alone is not wholly responsible for *The Terrible Murder of Kenneth Pitt*. Hers is only the seed of the crime. First seeking advice from their Moog-playing A&R friend Ralph Mace, he suggests she and David speak to his label's General Manager, Olav Wyper, who listens sympathetically to their grievances. David explains that Ken is more than a friend. He's anxious about severing their management contract, but for the good of his career he must. Olav tells them they're going to need the help of a good lawyer. David says he doesn't know any. Can Olav recommend one?

He can. The first candidate that pops into Olav's head is a weird young chap he recently lunched with at the Tratt. Big hair. Odd dress sense. Like a Victorian with an afro. But keen. Very keen.

Olav speaks, and it's from his lips that David Bowie first hears the name Tony Defries.

THE TERRIBLE MURDER of *Kenneth Pitt* occurs less than half a mile from Pitt's Manchester Street apartment. As Ken reclines contemplating from afar his meticulously ordered volumes by André Gide, he is wholly unaware that David is nearby, in an office in Cavendish Square, sitting beside Angie and contemplating the long fleshy schnoz of Ken's imminent executioner. The schnoz bulges beneath two heavy-lidded eyes, their pupils large and steady like a couple of black holes sucking in all available light. Orbs that penetrate everything but themselves are penetrable by nothing. The unflinching eyes and inquisitive schnoz match the formal furnishings of a solicitor's firm behind the listed Edwardian façade of Harcourt House, W1. Less so the haircut. A bubble of black frizz mushrooms from scalp and temples like a wire-wool crash helmet. It is tricky to place an age on such an assembly: neither young nor old, not fully from the present nor the past.

Like the emperor Nero in a wig from *Hair*. This is the hitman who will kill Ken for David. This is Tony Defries.

Defries is 26, Jewish, raised south of the river, though he'll tell reporters he's from Shepherd's Bush because it implies a romantic street apprenticeship of artful dodgery that Croydon doesn't. Rule Number One in the Gospel According to Tony Defries: never let the facts of humdrum reality prevent the selling of outrageous fantasy.

His knowledge of music is tone-deaf but when it comes to the fiscal mechanics of its industry he has perfect pitch. Defries hears poetry in percentages, cadenzas in clauses and harmony in hidden assets. His teeth were cut on years of acute observation in the shadow of his master, Allen Klein, and his capacity to retain, retrieve and recite detailed information is so thorough as to seem inhuman. Under that coarse hair and behind those deceptively slow eyes spins an encyclopaedic mental Rolodex of names, dates and decimal points. Rotate to B. Bowie, David. It means nothing to Defries. 'Space Oddity'? The song rings a distant bell but not the face that sang it. The sad and pitiful face that Defries now sees staring back at him over his desk – straggly hair, sunken cheeks and teeth that would embarrass a mangy dog. His fingernails are bitten to the cuticle and his clothes, though clean, fold scruffily around his bones. Angie, on cue, does her best impression of a carnival barker for The Greatest Show on Earth but the vision of David is the vision of a pathetic orphan begging for shelter. Which, as Defries hears it, is exactly what he is.

The problem David spills is bread and butter to Defries. Elementary ball-breaking of the sort Klein taught him in his first morning on the job. He lets David do most of the talking, listening to the sorry tale of his binding contract with Kenneth Pitt. *Poor little chap*, thinks Defries. *He's got himself in a terrible mess.*

David finishes his story with a puppy-eyed sigh. Angie's is the bayonet gaze demanding action. Defries allows them the punctuation of a moment's deliberative silence. Then, leaning back in his chair, hands pressing fingertips together in a cradle, he breaks it in a voice smooth and unhurried so no syllable could ever be misheard.

'I can get you out of your contract.'

The words splash in David's skull like raindrops after a drought. Rain becomes tears. David weeps.

Outside, the plane trees tremble with silent sympathy as West End traffic hums, stopping and starting between the traffic lights. In Manchester Street, a teddy named Bobby stares dead-eyed at the bedroom ceiling in mute agony. In the Italian café on the corner a radio plays and a black voice sings.

Farewell is a lonely sound.

David wipes his eyes. Angie and Defries clink smiles like wine glasses. Smiles that taste blood in the air.

The first thing he must do, counsels Defries, is to write and inform Ken that he is no longer his manager. David mouths OK with a compliant nod. Defries slides a blank sheet of paper across the desk and hands him a pen. Then dictates.

'I have been advised . . .'

HIS NEW DRUMMER still wounded, David continues to gig alone. Blind man's buff scheduling catapults him to a northern cabaret casino in Stockport to support Barclay James Harvest. He savours a couple of meat pies from the local chippie, serenades the progressive apostles of Greater Manchester, misses his train and ends the night curled up alone on a bench in Stockport railway station, stomach digesting gristle, mind digesting gristlier business to come as the North-West snores with disinterest towards dawn.

Dawn brings headlines of a newly post-Beatles world where Gypsy Rose Lee is dead and a plot to kidnap Princess Margaret's 8-year-old son as ransom to free the Kray twins is foiled. The number 1 single is 'All Kinds Of Everything' by Dana, an 18-year-old Irish Catholic schoolgirl who recites the rosary every day with her manager, a 48-year-old headmaster who will shortly resign his post so he can dedicate himself full-time to her career. Within a week – *Hail Mary, full of grace!* – Dana will sack him.

On the red-eye train to Euston, David mutters advance prayers for similar sins.

A DOORBELL RINGS in Manchester Street. The executioner's song. Ken has been expecting it; judging from the frozen rictus of button-eyed despair, so has Bobby. They're here on the stroke of 5 p.m. Just as had been arranged a few days earlier when Ken answered his phone and found himself being told on behalf of Messrs Godfrey, Davis & Batt of Cavendish Square to expect a visit from a Mr David Bowie, who he quite obviously knew, and a Mr Anthony Defries, who he most certainly didn't. The date and time specified, the caller hung up, leaving Ken and Bobby to count their last desperate days together until the bell rang and the axe fell. The bell now having rung, Ken presses the entry buzzer to allow the axeman and his accomplice into the building and up the stairs. A knock on the outside door. A condemned gulp. Resigned, Ken opens it and puts a face to Fate.

His first thought is that Fate has an enormous schnoz. Behind the schnoz, David squeezes his lips into a watery grin. Ken's return is even wetter. The mouth curls but behind the lenses the eyes whine.

Et tu, Bowie?

It is the first time Ken has laid eyes on David since he sent him the letter reading: *I have been advised.* Ken had eventually responded, writing that he was not in any position to relinquish their standing contract but that he was willing to discuss ways in which they *might*. David never replied and passed the letter straight to Defries, who was amused if unruffled by the contents, having already passed sentence of death upon its author.

This, the killing time.

Ken ushers them inside: Defries, formally suited and tied; David, casually satined and tatted. They sit, David's force of habit slumping on the edge of the green chaise longue. He is silent and remains so, a ventriloquist dummy at rest while Defries proceeds to speak for both of them. Ken is half listening, half preoccupied, wondering who or what is the lifeless waxwork of the boy he used to know as David staring blankly at a fixed point on an invisible horizon somewhere on the opposite wall. Ken thinks he might be stoned. No. Not stoned. Pretending to be stoned. Just another bad 'mime'. Sitting there as if he's not there and if he's not there then it's not happening. That way David doesn't have to say or do anything. Just be there not being there, not looking at Ken, not registering the hurt, not feeling guilty or cruel or spineless or disloyal or sad. Not feeling anything at all.

Defries finishes the deed with measured legalese. Ken aims a farewell glance at the handsome coward now stiffly upright on his chaise longue, knowing it will be his memory's last bitter portrait of David in Manchester Street. Suffering is one very long moment.

The execution complete, Defries and David rise and leave. Before reaching the door, David hesitates. The eyes flicker, a hand extends and a tiny voice croaks.

'Thank you, Ken.'

They touch flesh. Pulse to pulse. Then untouch just as quickly. The door closes behind them and David is gone. Never has Ken's door looked more shut.

Ken walks over to the window where he stands watching David and Defries make victorious strides down the street until both are out of sight. His eyes fix on the spot where they vanish and stay there blinded by the after-image of the final frame. For Ken, the very long moment never ends.

THIRTEEN

THE FLOORS OF HADDON HALL faintly shake with dull repetitive rhythm. Nothing syncopated, just a frantic bang-bang-bang. The tempo of tools and industry, man and materials, hammer and nails, echoing from down below, in the cellar next to the building's basement flat. Not 50 years ago the space was stacked floor to ceiling with fine wines to be fetched and served to dinner guests of the suburban bourgeoisie. An empty chamber, unkempt and unused, until Tony, the son of a carpenter with sawdust in his veins, chose to renew its dead stone with a second inner skin of wood. He constructs a room within a room, packing the thin gap between with egg boxes to soundproof a practice space where he, David, Mick and Woody can create and perfect their noise with minimum nuisance to the neighbouring flats. It is just big enough to fit kit, amps and instruments but with the added cram of four bodies becomes a cauldron of claustrophobia. So is the music they fashion here.

The music is music of the underground. Born in a condemned cell below street level, a music that knows no daylight. Dark, imprisoned, paranoid, angry and suffocating. Some of it like an earthworm burrowing deep down, weaving through clay, roots and mycelium, slow cold-blooded music made of insects, moss and rotten vegetation. Some of it like molten lava, white-hot, solemn and sulphuric, music that flows in hissing black slabs from the centre of the earth on a volcanic tide of destruction. All of it unsettled, volatile, wound-licking and sad.

Its blacksmiths are three men who think they have an idea what they're doing and one who doesn't. The one who doesn't is the one supposed to be navigating their way through the subterranean murk, but David is a leader without a lead. He has only a couple of complete songs. Everything else is scraps, sketches and nameless scree, vapours of inspiration which the others must solidify into songs of form and force. With his arranger's ear, Tony starts to create order from David's chaos, his basslines plotting the route with commanding clarity. Mick adds definition, bold outlines and forked lightning. Woody rivets everything in place, sticks splitting anvils like Siegfried in hard, strong and steady strokes. The sound is more dense and dramatic than David could have conceived alone but now it is his to steer. Only, with his hands unwilling to take the wheel, it must follow the drag of its own weight into the infernal depths.

Time is against them. There is a tight budget and as tight a recording schedule for David to make his next album. He's been gibbering to the press about the new record being mostly acoustic but when Tony marshals him to start work at a change of studio, Advision, round the corner from the BBC amongst the Marylebone rag trade, all they have are these brutal noises from the bowels of Haddon Hall. It becomes a perverse game of cause and effect. Heavy tunes begetting heavy words begetting heavier tunes. David keeps his cards close to his chest. Tony suspects it's because the cards are blank. Most of the songs don't have names because they still don't have words. For Tony, it is all very unDavid. But then David has become very unDavid. He is no longer the David who turns up with ready words and music, the 12-string troubadour playing his songs through from beginning to end for the other musicians to fall in and follow. He is now the unDavid of abstraction and distraction. Of ill-fitting jigsaw pieces left for others to slot together, of half-ideas and whims of whims, of working titles that stay working titles even when the work is finished. Of cannabis-scented tardiness arm in arm with Angie, of shopping bags and antiques and talking about their fabulous finds in a lovesick haze of *oochie angie pangie davie wavie grumpy uncle tony moany koo-ka-choo* baby babbling. An unDavid lost in everything except music.

★

THE PRISON SENTENCE without parole called yesterday tugs him to the Talk of the Town on the edge of Leicester Square where bronze statuettes of Euterpe, the Greek muse of music, await engraved and ready to be collected by the winners of the Ivor Novello Awards. This year's Oscars of the pop world have been selected by a judging panel including disc jockeys Pete Murray and David Jacobs, Anita Harris, resident singer on ITV's *David Nixon's Magic Box*, the *NME*'s News Editor Derek Johnson and the songwriter Lionel Bart. Only one of the above is an alcoholic homosexual whose casual frolics include tonight's recipient of the Certificate for Originality, David Bowie.

A strange world of tuxedos and cummerbunds, collar dresses and diamonds, Matt Monro and Roger Whittaker, syrup and religion. Frankie Vaughan is backed by the Daughters of the Cross to bother heaven and hippodrome with 'Peace Brother Peace'. From one of the tables a woman stands up and screams 'What about Cambodia?' and is abruptly bundled out of the building. It is a night of ugly opposites, finishing with Dana singing about the Lord as an appetiser for the climax of Ginger Baker's Air Force smashabanging for 15 torturous minutes. The dickie-bowed stick their fingers in their ears and wave handkerchiefs in mock surrender. On Mount Olympus, so does Euterpe.

Somewhere between holy cack and cacophony, David appears, a poor wayfaring stoner lost in respectable space, clinging to his acoustic guitar in the dark floral silk shirt he married Angie in and clashing pink trousers. He must sing live accompanied by Les Reed and His Orchestra who attempt to launch 'Space Oddity', his winning original song. But the Stylophone sound is a pantomime fart and the solo a jagged joke that makes David splutter. The song's pathos explodes and 'Space Oddity' plummets to earth in the wreckage of 'Kumbaya' with strings by Disney. All this extravagant self-abuse is televised live by satellite to America where it's afternoon in Los Angeles and teatime in New York – not that anyone is tuning in to see David; not that anyone who does will remember him.

For his trouble, he doesn't even receive a proper Ivor statuette. His Certificate for Originality is literally that: a piece of paper informing David Bowie that in the esteemed opinion of the singer from *David Nixon's Magic Box* he ought now consider himself 'original'.

★

103

AN ORIGINAL CATASTROPHE. A military plane has crashed in the sea off the South Coast carrying three nuclear weapons. Two are lost in the depths while a third washes up by a pier where the owner of a penny arcade mistakes it for an old war mine and plans to dismantle it for spare parts. Only when he shows signs of radiation poisoning does his daughter call the men from *Doomwatch*.

They're a sullen-looking bunch, brows ploughed by the daily stresses of battling chemical warfare, man-eating rats and pandemic viruses apart from Toby Wren. Scientist by day, smoking neckerchiefed dandy by night, a skinny Englishman with topaz eyes and a snow-white tan, Byron handsome but Sherlock gaunt, beautifully human yet coolly extraterrestrial. Toby is why schoolgirls stay up past their bedtime on a Monday evening to be fed delicious dreams of his topaz eyes bearing down on them, spinning off a luminous glow just like those new Coty make-up ads. *'The electric eye.'* Toby Wren is Extravalash for the loins.

Tonight, Toby saves the world by defusing the bomb on the pier with three minutes to spare before the late n . . . *oh, shit!*

'There's another wire!'

Bang goes the bomb, the pier, Toby and his electric eyes. Britain pisses and shrieks and the search for the Seventies Valentino is over.

Agony pours into Television Centre by the sodden sackful.

'If this letter is tear-stained it is the BBC's fault. You have no soul.'

Toby Wren is dead. The fact actor Robert Powell isn't cannot stem the rivers of Coty streaking teenage cheeks from Bolton to Bournemouth. The man has killed the kids and Powell's pin-up now hangs over their beds like a crucifix.

Martyrdom is the Seventies' new rock'n'roll.

THE NAME ABOVE the title is missing from the picture. Work on David's album is nearly over but David remains its phantom star. There is only so much Tony can do without him. The tracks are all ready to be presented. David's loose scraps have been smoothed, tidied, framed and mounted, their gelatinous bodies given shape and volume, their verses softened and choruses hardened, their colours enriched with witchy woodwind and flying-saucer Moog, their weak links soldered strong by the white heat from a Spring Bank Les Paul. When not playing, Mick is still learning. Tony shows him how to convert the tunes in his head into crotchets on the page so Mick can start to score his own arrangements. He studies the mixing console like it's the periodic table, memorising every button, dial and fader, row by row, making note of what gets pushed every time Tony performs a magic trick. But there's only so much swotting a Yorkshireman can do.

When David does turn up on set he is a meticulous diva. Everything must be just so. Tony, Mick and Woody take comfort; this means he must be serious about 'Cyclops', 'Black Country Rock', 'The Man Who Sold The World' and other tunes still missing lyrics. 'Black Country Rock' becomes 'Black Country Rock' because David can't think of anything else to sing about and does so in a sheep-dipped gargle unmistakably intended to mimic Marc. Nobody present is sure why he does this and nobody present is terribly pleased that he has. 'The Man Who Sold The World' becomes 'Saviour Machine' and stabs an old wound by regurgitating a melody from a past David's still trying to forget, when he and Hermione – oh, Christ, *Her-mi-on-ee* – sweetly chirruped their 'Ching-A-Ling' song. Then, on the very last day of mixing, David finishes the lyrics to another forlorn instrumental, clapping its castanets to the over-under-sideways sobs of Mick's hypnotic Yardbirding. Rummaging in his waste bin, he retrieves the discarded title 'The Man Who Sold The World'. Rummaging in his soul, he retrieves what first he thinks is a hollow replica of himself until he realises that maybe this gazeless horror actually is his real self and it's he who all these years has been its hollow replica. He sings a description to fit the music and to everyone's relief David's album is complete. It never crosses anyone's mind to ask if he's feeling all right.

Even if they did, could his hollow replica answer?

FOURTEEN

NEW STARS FOR 1970. From California, Norman Greenbaum, a self-sufficient hippie living on a farm with two horses, a puppy, a parakeet, goats, chickens and several cats. He grows his own courgettes and once wrote a song about an aubergine that ate Chicago. That wasn't a hit but his 'Spirit In The Sky' is and spends two weeks at number 1 praising Jesus. The son of Jewish refugees, Norman says he isn't really religious 'in the church sense', only 'in a way of life in food and thought'.

From France, the 37-year-old *femmes au foyer*'s favourite Sacha Distel wins the UK chart race against rival versions of 'Raindrops Keep Falling On My Head'. It earns him *19* magazine's swoonsome headline 'Sacha the Smasher' and a *Mirabelle* quiz to find his name among the following blanks.

$$S - - H - \quad - I - T E -$$

From Canada, the troubadour's troubadour Leonard Cohen has shaken enough Che Guevara posters on the walls of student digs to sell out two nights at the Albert Hall. He enjoys neither, confessing amazement that young women should still bother to wait outside his hotel room afterwards. 'I don't want them,' sighs Len, 'but sometimes my body takes over and I have them. But that's not me doing it – it's my body.' And on he tours, touching perfect bodies with his mind or fucking them daft without it.

From a bedsit in Hampstead, *Jackie* magazine's quest to 'Meet the Goodlookers' unearths a 'tall, gentle, modest and very, very shy' specimen named Nick Drake. Evidently too shy to be a pop star, Drake's two albums to date have been bought by approximately no one. 'I couldn't tell you what my songs are about,' he evaporates, safe in the knowledge his twain and *Jackie*'s shall never meet again.

From bad to worse, Edison Lighthouse are crucified on stage in Glasgow trying to tour without Tony Burrows, the studio voice of their only hit record. Living an unsustainable lie, the group suffer the consequences and book their suite in pop oblivion. The mercurial Burrows himself is now half the culprit in a duo called The Pipkins, responsible for the brain-dead ragtime 'Gimme Dat Ding'. 'It's about a metronome that's lost its ding,' Burrows tells Radio Luxembourg's *Fabulous 208* magazine. The record reaches number 6 in a country so sickened by daily scares of 'BOVVER BOYS' and 'PAKI-BASHERS' it gladly laps up the Saturday-night anaesthetic of *The Black and White Minstrel Show*. These are desperate times.

'Do faces and names really matter?' asks Mr. Bloe. 'I don't think that they do. People buy discs like "Mr. Bloe" simply because they like the noise.'

'Groovin' With Mr. Bloe' is a much better noise than 'Gimme Dat Ding' though Mr. Bloe is no more corporeal a pop entity than The Pipkins. Mr. Bloe was very nearly Elton John until the last minute when his ivories were replaced by those of pianist Zack Laurence. The tune, an American cover, kicks Larry Adler around the sprung dance floor of Wigan Casino in ever-decreasing circles. It doesn't quite make number 1, but to a thousand and one love-bitten youth clubs stinking of Wood Nymph and Woodpecker cider 'Mr. Bloe' is the new national anthem.

There are songs, there are singers, there are tunes and there are tunemakers but one summer into the Seventies there are still no real superstars.

'The word "super" has been misused,' sniffs progressive organ torturer Keith Emerson. 'It was quite relevant when applied to people like Elvis Presley who was the first to be called a superstar. But now it's applied to everything – washing-up liquids, hair shampoos – who wants to be put on the same level as that?'

★

THE POSTMAN RINGS the bell of Flat 7, Haddon Hall. He waits. A minute passes in stutters of birdsong and the murmur of occasional traffic. Finally, the door clicks, opening to an arrow slit just big enough for David to brace all the daylight he dare. It takes a few seconds for his eyes to blink into focus.

'Mike?'

He opens the door wider.

'Come in.'

Mike follows David inside, slipping his coat and postbag off his shoulders as he's shown into the living room where the television is on with the sound turned low. David disappears into the kitchen, returning with two mugs of coffee to find Mike flicking through a copy of *Picture Show* magazine he's picked off the carpet. David has stacks of old film mags and annuals. Cowboys, swashbucklers, screen gods and goddesses. On his mantelpiece now sits a framed portrait of Greta Garbo. Divine, alien, unreachable. The ultimate star.

'You were saying . . .'

David and Mike pick up a conversation from where they'd left it the last time. The last time was the last time Mike was on the second delivery down Southend Road when he loaned David his Andy Warhol book, an original American Factory exhibition catalogue. The time before that could have been in the back of The Three Tuns where Mike joined in at the Arts Lab, up on stage with Cliff Penge and the SE20s. Mike also designed posters for the Lab. He was an artist, cartoonist and occasional poet long before he donned a mail bag, and still is. He only took the postie job thinking it would work out so he'd have lots of spare time to draw and paint. But the pay isn't great and his nights have been hijacked by insomniac shifts bag-tying at the main sorting office opposite the war memorial where the more debauched posties kill time setting up projectors in the back to grunt over dirty one-reelers. It's all going on in Beckenham – the suburb that never sleeps for fear of what it might dream.

The only perk of the job is when Mike is given the late-morning delivery route including Southend Road. He always leaves Haddon Hall to the end so he can pop in and see David and Angie, sometimes sitting and chatting to them on the end of their bed surrounded by hastily strewn clothes and the creative detritus of David's rough jottings. David and Angie are both fans of Mike's art, especially his Arts Lab poster design with the exploding head, and the drawing of his friend, Douglas, who wants to be a woman so he asked Mike to make him a wedding picture of himself, as a man, marrying himself, as a woman, both wearing dresses. Angie loved it so much she practically exploded.

'I was saying?'

Mike's conversation with David started about nine years ago behind a hedge in the corner of the playing field of Bromley Technical School for Boys. Smokers' Corner. Mike was in the fourth year, David in the third, but he was the kind of boy who preferred hanging out with older boys like Mike to listen to his stories about Ken Tapley.

Ken was a typical suburban boy, just like them, who became a rock'n'roll singer signed to Decca Records, the same label as Billy Fury and Anthony Newley, who'd one day sign David. Between puffs, Mike would go into great detail about Ken, his background, his music and all sorts of personal gossip that you would never read about in *NME*, *Melody Maker* or any of the main music papers. Mainly because Ken Tapley didn't exist. Ken was purely a product of Mike's eager pencil and overactive mind. A fictitious rock'n'roll star. David thought this was great. Just invent a character and talk about him like he's real so people might actually believe he is. Even if he's just a scribble in an exercise book and a break-time chimera for brown-fingertipped schoolboys.

The other funny thing about Smokers' Corner was that David never actually smoked back then. He'd just hang around, inhaling the tarry mist of Mike and the fourth years' Player's Weights, talking about his brother's jazz records.

'My brother Terry's got that.'

Terry, Terry, Terry. Always Terry. It was all little David used to talk about back then. LPs by Dexter Gordon and Charlie Parker. Books by Kerouac and Ginsberg. Terry had the lot. David spoke like a kid older than his years and nobody who heard him was in any doubt as to the beat godhead responsible.

'My brother Terry.'

But that was before the ground cracked and the sky caught fire. David doesn't mention Terry much these days. He only tells Mike that he's in

The Cane, which is all the information Mike needs not to ask any more. They've enough other things to discuss.

'About Anthony Newley?'

Last time David had been talking about Anthony Newley. Given half a chance he usually does. *The Strange World of Gurney Slade*. He was 13 when Rediffusion first showed it on Saturdays at 8.35 until they shoved it past bedtime; 16 when they repeated it on Friday nights, 10.15, before the late news. David's been living in Gurneyland ever since.

Tick-tock, tick-tock.

Gurneyland is anywhere, where anything can happen. It's up there in your mind, in your head. It's where once upon a time Mike found Ken Tapley and where everyone can be anyone they like. That's why Gurneyland is the most wonderful place in the whole world.

'You really should hear his compositional work.'

Mike is amused. Down at the Arts Lab, David serenaded the *IT* heads with Biff Rose and Jacques Brel but he didn't dare sing anything by Tony Newley, even though he'd spent the best part of the first five years of his recording career trying to sing *exactly* like Tony Newley. This was the direct consequence of having been told the secret of Gurneyland when his young ego was only half-formed and still much too pliable. Now he's a prisoner of his own fantasy. So free to be whoever he likes that he sometimes forgets who he is in the first place. And when memory fails, if nothing else, in Gurneyland David can always be Tony Newley.

Fol-de-dee!

Mike shares his love of *Gurney Slade*, and *Idol on Parade*, an Elvis-spoofing piss-take of Britain's rock'n'roll no-hopers lined up for national service starring Newley as Ken Tapleyesque khaki boogie boy Jeep Jackson. But he confesses he mainly knows Newley's singles. The early hits: 'Why?', 'Do You Mind', 'Strawberry Fair', 'Pop Goes The Weasel'.

David's missionary impulse sends him down on his knees rifling through his records. When he stands up again he's brandishing three of his cherished Newley LPs.

'Here,' he says, handing them to Mike. 'You can borrow these if you like.'

Mike takes the records, gathering them in his lap, inspecting front and back covers one at a time.

The Genius Of Anthony Newley. Black, impressionistic, serious. 'Every once in a while a truly great artist emerges – an artist whose gift makes people remember his talent all their life.' Crikey.

In My Solitude. White, minimal, existential. 'When Anthony Newley sings you find you must stop what you're doing and listen.' Songs called 'Winter Of My Discontent' and 'I'll Teach You How To Cry'. Looks very sombre.

Peak Performances. No sleeve note. Some of these tunes Mike recognises. 'Why?', 'Weasel', 'Strawberry'. The hits and more.

'It's got a great sleeve,' says David.

Newley sits in front of a dressing-room mirror in a black leotard greasepainted in his Littlechap clown face, his right hand touching the mirror like Michelangelo's *Creation of Adam*. In the mirror the finger extends to the opposite reflection of Newley without make-up, dressed in jacket, shirt and tie. The back cover is the same but flipped: Newley in his everyday clothes touching the mirror staring back at Newley the clown. Which is the actor and which is the character? Where does reality end and Gurneyland begin? Who is pretending to be who?

'Yes,' says Mike. 'It has.'

Mike takes the albums away with him and spends the next few weeks between energy-sapping postal shifts at home in Penge, listening to heavy words of love and loneliness Bow-belled into Cockney opera over swooning strings and gayest glissandi. All those twisted vowels, the As garrotted to Is. *'Children play their gime.'* The histrionic, wailing crescendos. *'Owwowwowwow!'* Now it all makes sense to Mike. He looks again at the cover of *Peak Performances* and sees Tony Newley touching the mirror, finger to finger, looking back at David. On the reverse he sees David touching the mirror, finger to finger, looking back at Tony Newley. Mike laughs, then catches sight of himself in his own bedroom mirror and stops laughing. Staring back at him, holding an LP by Tony Newley, he sees the startled face of Ken Tapley.

THE GHOSTS of lingerie dummies hear the ping of the elevator bell then watch unseen as the doors slide open to reveal two thin shaggy-haired creatures: one probably a man, one probably a woman, possibly the other way round. A sign reading Gem Productions tells David and Angie they're in the right place. They're greeted by Jan, the foxy receptionist forever in hotpants, who takes them through to an office where a thickset man with twinkly eyes, an even tan and a musketeerish moustache beseeches them to make themselves comfortable. This is Laurence Myers.

They've met once before, at the Talk of the Town, the night David picked up his Novello certificate. That was purely social. This is business. Defries's business. He's not present, but it's because of Defries that David and Angie are here in Laurence's office. He needs David to like Laurence and Laurence to like David, which means for David's sake he also needs Angie to like Laurence and Laurence to like Angie. If everyone gets along famously then all of Defries's careful strategising will have paid off. But only if.

Having dispensed with Ken, Defries has stepped up as David's new manager. The catch: this will only succeed if Defries leaves his law firm and joins up with an existing music management company like Gem. So he makes Laurence a bold offer. He'll bring David to Gem to sign up as one of their artists. In return, Defries will join Gem as a partner. This way David gets a new manager and the financial backing of an established production company, Defries gets to handle Bowie's affairs, a basic wage and a 20 per cent stake in Gem, and Laurence gets a new artist in David, a new business partner in Defries and with it a new in-house legal expert. Laurence agrees, in theory. *If* it all works out.

David and Angie are here to see if it can. Laurence tells David he loves 'Space Oddity' and thinks he's a good songwriter. For Laurence, pop is all about the song, not the singer. Find the right song, give it to the right person, stick them in the studio, get it heard on the radio, and the public will take care of the rest. It's how the minds of Mike Leander and Tony Macaulay work, and how Laurence's works. He thinks of David as a writer, not a star, and looking at David across his desk he doesn't see anything to alter that opinion. His clothes are floppy, his skin waxy and his hair a slept-in feminine tumble past his shoulders. He and Angie could be brother and sister, or sister and sister, or two very delicate brothers. One and the same apart from the volume: David, the gentle murmuring flute; Angie, the crashing timpani.

David leans forwards and picks up a sign on Laurence's desk.

ART FOR ART'S SAKE. MONEY FOR FUCK'S SAKE.

Then laughs, teeth glinting in the sunlight through the blinds like a necklace strung with bits of broken tile.

'I like that. I'll bear it in mind.'

David is playfully playing into Laurence's hands when Laurence closes the deal without even realising.

'You know, you really remind me of Tony Newley.'

David swoons.

'Really?'

That's odd, blushes David, because Newley is his all-time hero. He'd only said so in *Mirabelle* last month. 'Which famous people would you like to meet?' they asked. 'Anthony Newley. I've admired him for many years,' said David. Asked the same question, Cliff said, 'Doris Day.'

'Oh, I *adore* Newley,' says Laurence.

And David melts in buttercups and oojahs.

Laurence tells him Newley is the artist he'd love to manage more than anyone else. In fact, he's such a fan he saw him on stage at the Queen's Theatre in *Stop the World – I Want to Get Off* three times. Yes, David. *Three* times.

Stop the world – David wants to climb on. Angie squeezes his knee and gives the nod.

Fol-de-dee!

Where does he sign?

HAROLD WILSON names the date! The first general election where 18-year-olds will be able to cross ballots. *Disc* magazine polls the country's newly eligible voters and asks who they'd like as their local MP. In first place, John Lennon. In second, Cliff. In third, Jimmy Savile since 'he has more genuine concern and is more active in helping people than all politicians put together,' says Sheila in Merseyside. Over 80 per cent of kids would not want hippies in power. Neither do the adults.

'What do you think this is?' rages Enoch Powell at his Wolverhampton hustings. 'A contest between a man with a pipe and a man with a boat?'

'Yes,' says the public, who, come the day, choose the Tory man with the boat, Ted Heath: Wilson, the Labour man with the pipe, is photographed leaving Downing Street by the tradesmen's entrance.

In Fleet Street, the *Sun* back the losing team but win the circulation war with 'THE GIRLS WHO GET OUR VOTE TODAY', their chief conductress of a thousand phwoars Lamb's Rum bird Caroline Munro. In Wolverhampton, Enoch doubles his majority. In Whitehall, Heath appoints Margaret Thatcher to her first cabinet post as Education Secretary. 'In The Summertime', Mungo Jerry, is number 1.

Serious and spotty fans of progressive rock complain it sounds like skiffle left over from the Fifties. Possibly the success of its jolly jug-band limp is a protest against serious and spotty progressive rock fans. It is the biggest-selling single of the year and cause for legitimate concern to Marc Bolan, who in the goaty throat of Mungo singer Ray Dorset hears what might be the sincerest form of flattery if not wholesale identity theft. Chief witness for the prosecution: the review in *Music Now*. 'Near-Tyrannosaurus Rex vocals from Mr Dorset.' The jury is in.

In Bromley, with a new single to promote, David and his band try to bring memories to a free festival in Shortlands before a crowd of 300 weekend hippies, skinheads and inquisitive mums and dads. He has retired the name of Hype and now wants Mick, Tony and Woody to be listed as the backing group Harry The Butcher. A scuffle breaks out near the stage but David and the band cleave on. According to the local paper, they steal the evening. If only Bromley's was the conscience of the world.

'Goodness knows what David is up to on this long, rambling, repetitive piece of nonsense.'

The *Melody Maker*'s verdict on the new single is shared by everyone except *Disc*, who bother to review it twice. 'Beautiful,' gushes his faithful altar maiden Penny Valentine. 'Very good arrangement and vocal,' adds fun-loving Tony Blackburn. With a *Woof! Woof!* from Arnold.

His label's marketing budget stretches in vain to a couple of press adverts.

DAVID BOWIE'S MEMORY OF A FREE FESTIVAL
IS A SINGLE YOU WON'T FORGET

Adverts that nobody remembers. Within a week, chart hopes extinct, the 'Memory' is lost.

★

THERE ARE NO MEMORIES among the living dead. Shuffling sad accursed clay people, their eyes like blown lightbulbs, burned filaments weakly recalling the strangers in their midst. Visitors from the world they left behind. Mothers, fathers, sisters, brothers, sons, daughters, friends and lovers come to see what's left of them. The wreckage of selves that haven't yet been eroded by prescribed psychic battery acid. Recognisable but charred ruins of what stood and spoke and lived and laughed before the carpet bombs of Largactil rained devastation. Bring them books and magazines and sandwiches and see what fire flickers in the ashes of the lost individual.

For some, the damage is too much to bear. They see a massacre of the innocents in a war that has no need for such heavy armoury. The dust of a fucked society brushed under its carpet: isn't that why they call it the loony *bin*? Human waste disposal. They can't burn them at the stake any more for being sons and daughters of Beelzebub, so they lock them away to be kept out of our sight and out of their minds. Suspended in agitation, constipation, infertility, drowned libido, excessive lactation, stopped menstruation, erectile dysfunction, man tits, dizziness, anaemia, seizures, tremors, erratic heartbeat, hallucinations and vomiting. *'Bringing relief to troubled minds.'* It is the only way. Apart from the *other* way.

Antipsychiatry. A primal scream among the choir of Sixties counterculture. Christened by the South African existential Marxist David Cooper, weaned by acid-popping Glaswegian psychiatrist R. D. Laing. Mewling in the beat presence of Ginsberg and Burroughs in the '67 Dialectics of Liberation international congress at the Roundhouse. Schooled in '68's revolutionary Antiuniversity established in Shoreditch. Clearing the field of all preconceptions regarding who, what and where we are. Demystifying the entire world as we 'know' it. Laing doesn't even like using the term 'schizophrenia' but knows he must 'since it is on the lips of so many'. He insists the schizophrenic must not be judged by our own 'sane' experience. Society may itself have become biologically dysfunctional, and some forms of schizophrenic alienation from the alienation of society may have a sociobiological function that we have not recognised.

This is why antipsychiatry advocates compassionate counselling, not medicated paralysis. They don't accept 'schizophrenia' as being a biochemical, neurophysiological, psychological fact. They regard it as a palpable error in the present state of the evidence to take it to be a fact. Nor do they assume its existence. Nor do they adopt it as a hypothesis. They propose no model of it. Capitalism, they say, simply puts profit before people, drugs before therapy, and so long as that remains the case 'schizophrenia' can never be treated.

Antipsychiatry is the answer, thinks Ronald's mum. Ronald is a friend of Mike not long alienated from the alienation of society: labelled schizophrenic, thrown in The Cane, blitzkrieged by chemicals. His mum has written to Laing who's agreed to help fight her son's case. Douglas's mum is also concerned – Douglas, Mike's friend who wants to be a woman. His mum argues if it makes her son happy to become her daughter then she doesn't see a problem with gender reassignment. Her son's psychiatrists tell her Douglas is insane.

Behind the net curtains of suburban Shortlands a Cane mutiny is brewing. Ronald's mum organises a public meeting in her front room to discuss better care and improved treatments for patients. She spreads the word to fellow relatives of the Coulsdon damned, hoping they'll support her fight against the hospital administration. As a friend of Ronald, and Douglas, Mike attends. Most of the faces he doesn't recognise. Except one. For a heartbeat Mike is surprised to see it. But then he remembers.

'My brother . . .'

There in Ronald's mum's front room, eyes alert and ears pricked, sits David.

FIFTEEN

FIVE YEARS. That's all Marc's got. He's made a Faustian pact with himself. Just five years to work this thing out. Five years from today, the day he's chosen to abbreviate his band name to the simpler T. Rex. And at the end of those five years, if he's dissatisfied, if he's failed, then he'll just have to resign himself to the fact that he's just not suited to the 20th century. 'Then I'll go to the country,' he decides, 'to explore my head.'

Five years begin on the first of July. A summer's Wednesday in Soho and Marc is back in Trident to start his fifth album with Tony, his first as T. Rex, assisted by the bodice-ripping palms of his new smouldering syncopator Mickey. It is Tony's first session with Marc since his last session with David. Much has changed in the interim. Haddon Hall is no longer Tony's home. For peace, privacy and sanity, he and Liz have just moved out to their own pad not so far away in Penge. He still sees David regularly, but right now Tony couldn't be happier to see Marc. He never needs to coax Marc. There's never anything unclear or half-finished begging for a second opinion because Marc never comes empty-handed. There's always a song, a riff, a groove or a poem, and even if there isn't, it won't take him a blink to pluck some fairy-tale jive and a silvery lick smooth as a T-Bird fin out of the ether convinced, as he is, of his own divinely inspired genius. Marc's ego always provides the spark. Tony's task is merely to fan the flames into a vibe inferno.

Marc has brought such a spark today. He wrote it only yesterday in his flat in Blenheim Crescent after a wasted afternoon's mope getting on June's nerves. She told him to stop idling and go in the other room and write a song, which he did. Then he completely forgot about it until this morning when he played it back to her. June thinks 'it's a gas' and he can't disagree. It's typical Marc. The jive: stone circles. The lick: Ford power-glide. Tony doesn't need to hear a dry run to tweak and arrange. Just roll the tape and let him blaze. Down in the live room Marc is strapped, picked, plugged, gained, toned and ready. Mickey tosses the hair from his eyes and tingles a tambourine. Up in the controls, Tony tests the levels.

'What's it called, Marc?'

'"Ride A White Swan". Call it "White Swan" for now.'

'OK. "White Swan", take one . . .'

Whoomph!

Marc's hand quick-draws and the air combusts. A sound from the past shocked into the present to electrify the future that might be Carl Perkins in the 25th century or a Sun 78 by Buck Rogers and The Tennessee Three or any other conceivable time slip between. But unmistakably the sound of rock'n'roll reborn in, and for, the Seventies. Not a revival but a clean slate, like Elvis, Buddy, Gene, Eddie, Bo, Chuck, Jerry Lee and Richard never happened until this happened, nor had any 'Roll-Over-Be-Bop-A-Blue-Suede-Bam-Boom-Boogie' ever shaken a jukebox until this subterranean Soho hour when the clock strikes one, two, three o'clock, four o'clock Marc. The same adolescent eureka of sex, fantasy and escape in voice, guitar and rhythm, its same words of love and magic now an Arthurian rap about druids, sunbeams and stars on foreheads *da-da-deeing* to a bouncing Barbarella rockabilly.

'Ride A White Swan' blinds with the gleam of ungraspably familiar stolen goods: of 'Peggy Sue's and 'Hello Mary Lou's, of the spoils from Scotty Moore and James Burton's crusades for the glory of Presley and Nelson. But just as they looted from Leadbellies, Blind Willies, Tee-Tots and Shake Rags, Marc, their star pupil, knows larceny is half the battle of originality. The tune is such a swag though the words are more peculiar to the old Bolan of babes, spells and cats, focused through his square-eyed love of *Catweazle*, his favourite new TV show about an 11th-century wizard who's accidentally zapped himself into 1970. Much like 'Ride A White Swan'. Ancient sorcery made modern miracle.

In less than three minutes the 'White Swan' is ridden. Marc hears Tony's voice through the talkback. 'Well, I got the sound. I was getting the sound with the tape echo just to make sure it would sound good that way.'

'Thank you, man,' says Marc. 'I want that sound, y'know?'

'You want it with the tape echo?'

Marc wants it with the tape echo. A simple song recorded with *Catweazle* electrickery but the greatest thing to happen so far to the Seventies. Maybe the greatest thing that ever *will* happen to the Seventies. Here, in a basement studio below St Anne's Court on 1 July 1970. History, raise your plaques – and do take care it's the right one. For this, the day, and here the place Marc Bolan, and none other, invented glam rock.

OUTRAGE IN BROADCASTING HOUSE. Memos from the highest brass demand the immediate dismissal of Radio 1's Kenny Everett from his Saturday morning show. Between his usual trademark 'zanies' featuring Crisp the Butler and a nymphomaniac granny, Kenny has sullied the moral standing of the BBC by daring to insult Mary Peyton, wife of the new Tory Minister for Transport, John Peyton. Following a news item about Mrs Peyton passing her driving test, Kenny withered she'd only done so after 'cramming a fiver' into the examiner's hand. It comes the same week *Melody Maker* runs an interview where Kenny describes Radio 1 as 'really revolting'. The casual slander of Mrs Peyton – upper-crusted daughter of a brigadier general, now wed to an old Etonian – is the last straw. Kenny must go.

Now £45 a week worse off, Kenny still has plenty to occupy his acid-bathed mind in the basement flat with rising damp in Holland Park he calls home, sharing it with a male macaw that he swears seems to suit the name Agnes, a Great Dane named Bosie, a parrot named Smokey, an 11-year-old Chihuahua named Bow Bells, a Yorkshire Terrier cross named Knickers, two cats – Spotly and Snuff, who keeps eating his aspidistra plant – various mice and a wife named Lee. He's also busy with his first series for London Weekend Television, *The Kenny Everett Explosion*, and should he need it there's always his spare office in the former corset showroom on Regent Street, now Laurence's Gem Productions, a shrewd move suggested by its resident number 1 shoveller, Tony Macaulay. It seemed a great idea when Kenny still had millions of Radio 1 listeners in his pocket: save time and shoe leather trying to plug him their new records by giving him an office of his own right there. Not so much now Kenny's no more than a manic squatter on LSD.

'When I said that Radio 1 was revolting I meant it,' Kenny insists, effervescent in defiance. 'It hasn't fulfilled the promise of the pirate stations.'

His sobering Saturday morning replacement is the BBC's youngest DJ, 21-year-old Noel Edmonds, who when not spinning the pick of the pops enjoys listening to Holst's *Planets* suite. 'Something will happen again,' predicts Noel when pressed for his thoughts on the future of pop. 'But the music scene needs to sort itself out. Otherwise we'll all be in a fix.'

THE POSTMAN RINGS twice on the bell of Flat 7, Haddon Hall.

Angie opens the door. 'MIKE? HI! COME ON IN.'

He follows her into the living room where David is strumming and the cathode ray humming. 'I've brought you back those Newley records.'

Mike hands over the three LPs. David is visibly pleased to see their safe return. The sacred tablets of Gurneyland. Mike wonders if, tit for tat, it might prompt David to remember that Andy Warhol Factory exhibition catalogue he borrowed a while ago. Looking around the room, Mike can't see it amongst the shelves of books, magazines and records. But David doesn't mention it and Mike decides that now isn't the time to bring it up. Not when David and Angie are both so excitable, each noisier and more animated than any of the blurry shapes behind them on the TV screen.

Things are apparently going very well for David. He tells Mike he has a new manager who's working on breaking him in America. He's also just finished his next album.

'It's fabulous,' says Angie as statement of fact.

'Do you want to hear it?' offers David. 'I can play you the tapes. I don't have a cover for it yet. Maybe when you hear it you'll get some ideas. Something like one of your Arts Lab posters?'

'OK.' Mike smiles. 'Yes, I'd love to. Thanks.'

The television is switched off. Angie reads the signals and gently excuses herself while David sets up his Revox reel-to-reel and loads a full supply spool, carefully threading it through the playback head onto the empty take-up. Mike remains sitting to attention on a straight-backed chair. David perches on the edge of the sofa. He lights a cigarette and nervously inhales. Leaning back, he presses play. Nothing is said for the next 40 minutes.

The tape spins.

David smokes.

Mike listens . . .

Track 1: 'The Width Of A Circle'

Starts a bit like 'Beck's Bolero' then wigs out like an Implosion all-dayer at the Roundhouse. David's worried about getting old and turning into a monster. God, God and more God. Something about Kahlil Gibran and getting laid. Five minutes and still raging. Suddenly all quiet. *'Progressive.'* Then more brimstone and smoking speakers. A bikers' boogie, thumbs in belt loops, waists winching back and forth, elbows bent, hair violently mopping thin air. Devil metal, hollers echoing from the ninth circle of hell and Zarathustra kettle drums. *Wow!* This. Is. HEAVY.

Track 2: 'All The Madmen'

Glum strums and creepy recorders. David's not quite right at all, is he? Cold mansions, Librium and lobotomies . . . bloody hell, he's singing about The Cane! *They're coming to take him away, ha-ha!* Spooky children's voices, deranged Wurlitzer and more 'Beck's Bolero'. This medication is HEAVY.

Track 3: 'Black Country Rock'

Sweetly sticky but – Christ! – that bass is bloody loud. David sings like a drowning lamb and Marc Bolan sharpens a talon. A tune half-empty balancing at the pop end of HEAVY.

Track 4: 'After All'
Sounds a bit like 'Space Oddity'. David's voice is beautiful but it's all so
dreadfully sad – that moaning Stylophone, the nightmarish pipe organ and
. . . *oh, by gosh, by gee*! It's 'Oh By Jingo!' Folky, funereal and HEAVY.

Track 5: 'Running Gun Blues'
Could be Eddie Cochran's 'Three Steps To Heaven' until all the corpses
and bloodshed and breaking gooks. David sings in one of his funny voices
and a twee organ wheezes. The tune is light, the artillery HEAVY.

Track 6: 'Saviour Machine'
One for the spaceheads in Dark They Were And Golden Eyed. David's
singing begs a standing ovation but the rest is rampaging robot prog. Very
rock opera but the scenery weighs HEAVY.

Track 7: 'She Shook Me Cold'
A fuse-blown mess of Jimi by The David Bowie Experience. Some chick
sucked and blew and smashed his head. A horrible noise more burned
black than bruised blues. Loud, ugly and HEAVY.

Track 8: 'The Man Who Sold The World'
Now *here's* a song. A guitar like a snake-charmed 'James Bond Theme'.
Once that mamba crawls in your ear there's no getting rid of it. Latin
rhythms and a chorus organ weeping '96 Tears'. Words about, well, who
knows? Not David. Dying harmonies and fade to black. This. Is. Fantastic.
The vibe, nevertheless, HEAVY.

Track 9: 'The Supermen'
More Zarathustra drums crawling like a diplodocus and Zarathustra words
bawled like a Dalek in orgasm. '*Oo-wah!*' sing the angels and Led Zeppelin
smell a rat. Beyond good and evil, David still isn't beyond Gurneyland
with his '*mad cele-bri-shuns*'. Well, *fol-de-dee*!

All very, very strange. All very, very HEAVY.

★

END OF TAPE. The silence that follows drops like a safety curtain. That wasn't what Mike was expecting. Not after listening to all those Tony Newley records. The words have shaken his thoughts into a flick-book of monsters, dark mansions, corpses, guns, supergods, machine men and men machines. He looks over at David and now pictures him touching a dressing-room mirror, finger to finger, with some hideous beaked monstrosity from Bosch's *Garden of Earthly Delights*. That was all very troubled.

Mike tells him. 'These are troubled songs, David.'

David knows Mike knows. He's just allowed Mike to peer inside his head and see all his locked-up terrors. The asylum of his Gurneyland. Only now he's written and sung about them, turned pain and paranoia into verse and chorus, given them a masked ball and invited the outside world within to waltz with his demons. He is a lunatic, exposed. He fidgets on the sofa. It was an honest remark: these *are* troubled songs. But he doesn't know how to reply. He fumbles in his defences and pulls out his funny Yorkshire accent.

'*Aye*,' he Ilkley Moors. '*That's me trouble list.*'

Mike blinks. *Me trouble list*? The phonetics roll around his skull like a loose ball bearing.

Me trouble list.

Meat rubble ist.

Me-trub-ol-ist.

'Metrobolist?' says Mike.

Metropolis! Yes! Fritz Lang. David's not seen it yet but he's read about it and seen images in books. Weimar science fiction. The nightmare shape of things to come. Maybe that's his album. *Mood Musik Für Maschinenmensch.*

'Metrobolist.' David grins, his voice back to Beckenham. 'I like that.' His head starts to nod. 'Yeah. That's the title. *Metrobolist.*'

The songs are still vibrating in Mike's head like the aftershock of walking free from a car crash when he returns home that night to start sketching ideas for the new record sleeve by his old friend from Smokers' Corner. An album by David Bowie called *Metrobolist*.

SIXTEEN

TREACHERY FERMENTS in Haddon Hall. The back bedroom vacated by Tony and Liz is now the plotters' den of Mick and Woody. For now is the summer of their discontent.

Since Woody arrived, Hype, or Harry The Butcher, or whatever David chooses to call them on any given day, have played just five gigs in four months. There have been no new radio sessions, no TV appearances and not a single magazine photo shoot. They spent one month of erratic studio visits making the album, but ten weeks after finishing it, they're still moping in Haddon Hall, counting the loose change in their jeans, arguing over the food kitty and who forgot to buy spuds.

The dream was to follow the yellow brick *turd* out of Hull to a magical rock'n'roll Oz. The reality is boredom, poverty and the odd rehearsal imprisoned in a cellar in suburban Kent. There are no sexy chicks screaming in the front rows because they're not playing to any front rows. They are not rich, not famous, and they are not rock'n'roll stars. They've only tobacco, beer, tea, toast, a roof over their heads, waning delusion and ulcers in their stomachs throbbing with something scarily like regret.

Mick feels the weight of every wasted second reminding him, yet again, he's made an enemy of fate. His head is an orchestra pit but his hands have nothing to conduct. All this – David, Angie, Haddon Hall and all tomorrow's promises after a crowd of 20 in a pub in Southend – is not enough.

Letters from home are siren calls beckoning him back to rocky ruin. He is loved. He is betrothed. The Humber wants him. Needs him. Mick hasn't forgotten the poisoned stink of creosote and diabolic squeak of the marker wheel, but he doesn't have to cloud-watch long to lose himself in rose-tinted reveries of the group he left behind. He invites Benny down again to spend a few days at Haddon Hall and the seeds of treason are sown. 'I want to reform The Rats,' Mick tells him. 'Keep it quiet, won't you?'

Woody is no less restless. He doesn't miss The Rats so much as life in a proper band. Regular work. Regular gigs. Late nights on A-roads laughing his lungs up in the back of the van. 'That was nice, Daddy! Can we do it again?' And once more round the roundabout.

David sees, hears and suspects nothing. He and Angie have too many intrigues of their own making house, whoopee and plans for his future. In the time it takes Mick to clatter around the small kitchen cooking a pan of curried beans they vanish without a word for meetings with the label to discuss the new record. It has been decided to release it in America first; if that means sending David on his maiden Stateside trip to promote it, he's happy to let Britain wait, along with his band who won't be going with him. Dizzy with dreams of Lexington 1-2-5, David is deaf to the conspiracy at hand on the other side of his bedroom wall.

The desertion, when it finally comes, is uncalculated. An automatic reflex on the long road heading north. David, in his Rover, leads the way to a gig in Leeds. Somewhere behind in another car are Mick and Woody. Both see it at the same time, waiting at a red light just past Wakefield. A small roundabout, two road signs, two arrows pointing two different directions.

The first is only a sign.

The second is a trigger.

They turn and look at one another.
Red light.
'Shall we?'
Amber.
'Fuck it.'
Green.
'Yeah!'
The car surges forwards, circling past the exit for Leeds, onwards and eastwards to where the river meets the sea and the air has a scent of acrid cocoa.

IN A WINDOW set between two Corinthian pilasters too high up to be noticed by the hordes herding to Hamley's below, a king peers down triumphantly from his new castle. A modest office with a desk, a telephone and a pigeon's-eye view of Regent Street, but to Tony Defries it's a throne of power. He claimed it with the managerial scalp of David, now a signatory to the court of Gem where Laurence has honoured his part of the bargain by installing Defries down the corridor from Tony Macaulay, Mike Leander and the ever-absent Kenny Everett as the latest starmaker in his Oxford Circus Brill Building. For Defries, the change in battlefield requires a change in armour. Freed from the formalities of suited legal eagling in Cavendish Square, he assumes the disguise of an agent of the Age of Aquarius. Open collars, big buckles, tight jeans and enough frizzy black hair to qualify as a member of The Flirtations. After years spent working with the music business now he *is* the music business.

For now it's only a lower rung. In real time it's 1970 but his inner clock of ambition is already wound up past 1984. One day, not this year but maybe next, he'll be the boss of his own Gem. Offices in London, New

York, Los Angeles. A global entertainment Reich. Bigger than Klein. Bigger than Colonel Tom Parker. The greatest manager of recording talent anywhere on earth. Such world-domination dreams are naked without a cigar and Defries already smokes the right cigar. In David, he also believes he has the right talent.

He tells David he thinks of him as a building. Like a skyscraper on New York's Sixth Avenue.

'You have the potential – in my hands, anyway – to create the income to make a building on Sixth Avenue. You are the beginning, potentially, of an Empire.'

David is left breathless by Defries's fairy tale: the little Brixton boy who woke up one day and found he was Manhattan real estate. Angie tells him it's true. She can see the view from the penthouse.

With David lost in the clouds, down on the ground Defries calmly divides and conquers. Angie is his ally. Even if she weren't, she'd be impossible to remove without the aid of the Royal Artillery and Defries needs her as much as she needs him to keep blanket-tossing David as high as they can.

The problem of Mick and Woody has solved itself. Defries had no interest in the group that was Hype. They were always Angie's pet motherly concern. She'd hustled their deal with the label to advance a few thousand pounds as a ruse to buy new equipment, and if the label never saw the money again that wasn't on his head. He'd already asked David to sack them. David clearly couldn't. The news of their absconding delights him.

Which leaves him only his namesake. The other Tony. Defries decides the best way to contain Visconti is to entice him to sign with Gem. He sells it as the best solution for all. David will be on the books as their artist; Tony, their producer. Defries will manage both, Defries will control both and Defries will take a sliver of both earnings.

It's the sliver that troubles Tony. In his honeyed proposition Defries makes the uncharacteristic mistake of overlooking two very important details. The first, that Tony has spent long enough in the industry to know when a fee has been skimmed and a percentage shaved. The second, that Tony's from Brooklyn where they spot weasel dealers at 20 paces and bump 'em before they reach 19. He spots Defries at 21. A regular illywhacker.

Tony nods and 'mm–hmm's as Defries tries to woo him with pecuniary lather, saying nothing until he and David are alone outside the Gem offices on the corner of Regent Street and Little Argyll. Then Tony says everything.

'Sorry, man, I can't work with him.'

David doesn't understand. 'Who?'

'Tony,' says Tony.

Did Tony say Tony?

'That guy just wants to make a ton of money. I want nothing to do with him.'

Then David twigs. He must decide: that Tony or this Tony.

'*Tony?* Oh, no . . . no, you've got him all wrong.'

Tony loses patience. 'Man, can't you see? Trust me on this. I've met his type before. He's not a manager. He doesn't care about you, or me. All Tony Defries cares about is Tony Defries.'

David's Empire State crumbles.

This Tony isn't quite done. 'There's no way I'm going to sign with him. Defries is bad news. If you want to stick with him, that's your choice. But if you do, I won't be able to work with you any more. I'm sorry, man. But that's just the way it is.'

David's eyes howl do not forsake me. All his lips manage is a soft mumble. 'Oh.'

Tony waits for words that never follow. The silence is a loud enough goodbye and lasts longer than either can stand. Tony ends it.

'I'll see you around.'

David watches the back of Tony's head bobbing away until it's lost in the West End crowd. For what might be a second but feels like a season he doesn't move. Then David turns, lights a cigarette and takes his first step of life in another direction.

IN AUGUST 1969 Woodstock let a genie out of a bottle which can never be put back. The stinking hippie summer festival is here to stay. In August 1970 the only festival on bitten teenage lips is the Isle of Wight: who'll be playing, how to get there and how to return without catching some medieval pelvic pox. The music papers offer polite cautionary advice to all young lambs ironing their denims ready for slaughter. Long before they reach the ferry, Isle of Wight 1970 is a self-fulfilling prophecy of the kind of articles the raciest girls' monthly, *Rave*, excels in. 'IS CHIVALRY DEAD?' 'WHAT ARE THE FACTS ABOUT V.D.?' 'WHAT ARE THE PSYCHOLOGICAL EFFECTS OF LOSING YOUR VIRGINITY?' The depressing answers to all three to be found on a Hampshire hillock at 3 a.m. wincing beneath a clammy oaf in a furry jerkin as Jim Morrison honks '*this is The End*'. Come Saturday morning, the site's barrier fence lies in matchsticks. This being British soil, the authorities blame the French. One reveller complains to the press that the locals treat them unfairly – 'like the maniacs who killed Sharon Tate': the locals point out that someone's just lobbed a hand grenade at the box office. Tony Blackburn is seen backstage and nobody quite understands why. By Sunday lunchtime the queue for the mercy bus out of Dodge is three miles long and one person slits their wrists: it was either this or stay and listen to Pentangle. The organisers had billed these five days of music as 'The Last Great Event', which it is. An apocalypse of common sense too much and too soon for the Seventies to risk ever happening again.

Summer ends, and with it a nation's last chance to make hay. Hark at them crying 'GOD!' for England and Saint George – Best for her, Susan for him. These, the sacred symbols of a 1970 sex life. He, the playboy rogue: all twinkles, hair and filth. She, the girl next door: all twinkles, hair and filth. Knowing the two Georges once dated drives common fantasy past the point of imaginable smut. Susan was last seen on the big screen as *Twinky*, a teenage nymphet who elopes with a writer of pornographic novels played by 48-year-old Charles Bronson. Best was last seen showing off his new millionaire bachelor pad with its own moat, a sunken bath and a television that rises and lowers from the chimney stack by remote control. The designer home is named Que Sera, as suggested by a devoted female fan. The house cost Best £35,000. The fan's reward is ten quid and an autograph: whatever will be will be. Susan has since been linked with an American actor. Best was last photographed with a Swedish nurse. Britain dreams, drools and turns the page to sordid tales of orgies, cuckoldry and murder in the Italian nobility. The tabloids take due care to run pictures of the dead marchesa's sun-lotioned bosom if only to illustrate the *bella bellas* some men will kill for. Cinemas high street and back street stifle in the heat of *Women in Love* and *The Wife Swappers* while the first 'sex supermarket' opens on Edgware Road. Its proprietor, Miss Ann Summers, aims 'to make sex education available to all'. And so, John Bull, to haymaking.

In terrace and semi, under stars and tent flap, morning, noon and night, bodies are expanding, bits engorging, parts glistening, heart rates accelerating, breath quickening, softness stiffening, lips billowing, blood pumping, tissue swelling, openings opening, insides gripping, colours changing, pinks reddening, whites purpling, muscles tensing, spasms spasming, contractions contracting, knuckles blanching, screams ripping, Vesuvius erupting, hallelujah chorusing.

And beneath a silver ceiling in Haddon Hall, life purposing. One year after the son lost the father two bodies entwine and separate as three.

Not so far away, on a rose bed of ashes, the roses bloom.

SEVENTEEN

THE BEATLES. Mick Jagger. Terence Stamp. Prince Michael of Kent. Lord Snowdon. Sammy Davis Jr. Even Bruce Forsyth. Royalty of rock'n'roll, showbiz and the crown itself have all been lured to an elite Mayfair boutique tucked behind Savile Row at number 17 Clifford Street to have their clothes rails blessed by the sartorial wizardry of one Mr Fish.

Mr Fish has risen to the height of fashion from its very depths in Wood Green, learning his trade in the Etonian outfitters of St James's and tailoring shirts for James Bond. The swing of the Sixties threw him into the loaded lap of a Sainsbury who agreed to back Mr Fish's own business selling a flamboyant wardrobe partly inspired by the colours, kanzus, tunics and textiles observed on a trip to Africa. The hangers of Mr Fish are the sound of *Sgt. Pepper* turned printed silk, chemise ruff and lilac cuffs. His garments are not 'Made by Mr Fish' but 'Peculiar to Mr Fish'. Among his peculiarities are the creation of the kipper tie, like the one Ronnie Corbett wore on his recent episode of *This Is Your Life*, and the man-dress, like the white-skirted tunic Jagger wore on stage in Hyde Park last summer.

David was there that day, watching Mick in his flouncy voile mini-dress reciting Shelley's stormy visions. He's since read all about Mr Fish, who's been profiled in *Jackie* and *Mirabelle* – 'tall, elegant, blue-eyed and fair-haired' – and splashed all over the tabloids after introducing this year's most outrageous Paris fashion to London. The midi for men.

'Englishmen are so lazy about changing out of their dull office clothes when they come home in the evening. I hope to change all that.' The *Mirror* says he's the assassin of trousers. Mr Fish believes the male midi-dress looks 'a bit Biblical' and predicts a future, 18 months from now, when most men will wear skirts. 'Clothes should be fun and exciting, not just a necessary protection. Dress to please yourself, throw in a bit of imagination and you can't lose.'

Where Bruce Forsyth treads David follows, and where David follows Angie leads. She is first to spy the Turin shrouds in the basement studio below Mr Fish's shop. Two ankle-length gowns: one salmon-pink velour with floral print and Chinese frogging across the breast; the other a soft Titian blue zipped up to a V-neck with an embroidered dragon on the back. She rips them off the rail and thrusts them at David, one in each hand, her face like the fourth of July.

'Wow,' David wows, then wows a very different sort of wow when Mr Fish folds his arms and tells them how much they cost.

'Try them on anyway,' urges Angie.

David disappears into the changing room. He emerges twice, one frock at a time, and twice Angie's heart leaps up her spine to ring her skull like a fairground high-striker. He looks like a medieval damsel stepped out from the frame of a Botticelli painting, or Garbo in her lamé dressing gown in *Grand Hotel*. Graceful, slender, girlishly boyish, lordly ladylike, both exotic prince and fairy-tale princess. He is beyond gorgeous.

Mr Fish agrees. David looks divine: no man has ever looked less of one in one of his garments. He reads Angie's mind, and before she can ask he obligingly lets pulchritude get the better of his pockets.

'I'll let you have them for 50 pounds apiece.' An 80 per cent discount. 'Just swear to me you'll tell people where you got them.'

A SHUTTER CLICKS in the lounge of Haddon Hall. David in his pink Mr Fish dress and knee-length boots reclines on a chaise longue covered in silken throws. Behind him, the lace curtains he and Angie dyed red, vases, plants and his antique folding screen. Scattered on the floor are two different packs of art deco playing cards. In his limp right hand, the king of diamonds. He raises a left hand, his wedding bangles sliding down his wrist as he strokes his scalp. The shutter clicks again.

The camera belongs to a young man named Keith. As 'Keef' or 'Marcus Keef' he's been working with Black Sabbath and Rod Stewart photographing and designing album sleeves for Philips' new underground label, Vertigo. Philips have commissioned Keef to take portraits for David's new album. It's David's idea to use his home as a fittingly idiosyncratic backdrop to unveil his new image, peculiar to Mr Fish, of a man allergic to smiling, the barbers and, most noticeably, trousers.

He repeats the same pose for Keef in both dresses, the plainer blue one offset by a black beret sloping at an angle atop his strawberry-blond curls. The hat is meant to summon the spirit of Greta Garbo, the new Madonna of his mantelpiece. He's been studying her portraits in thriftshop books and old film magazines for weeks, a crash course in star quality from fame's ultimate mistress of mystique. In every publicity still, a masterclass in how to position the hands, how to tilt the chin, how to sweep the hair, how to part the lips, how to lower the lids and arch the eyebrows, how to smoulder, how to swoon, how to be fire, how to be ice, how to be both, how to gaze into the lens with eyes so intensely true they could X-ray to the marrow of God. Every angle a sculpture. Every frame a work of art. The absolute enigma of absolute beauty condensed in two syllables. GAR–BO.

David has Keef at Philips, Garbo had Clarence Sinclair Bull at Metro-Goldwyn-Mayer. She wouldn't have her official portraits taken by anyone else. In April 1932, aged 26, three years older than David is now, she sat for Bull in costumes from her new film, *As You Desire Me*, including a sailing outfit with a black beret. This is David's muse as he lies back while Keef clicks away: a skinny man of 23 in a blue dress with alabaster skin, long wavy hair and mad mismatched eyes staring into an unknown future, hoping for the day when absolute beauty condensed in two syllables will spell the name of BOW–IE.

DIB COCHRAN & The Earwigs are loose. Marc and Tony's secret experiment, 'Oh Baby', is finally rung out by Bell Records. 'It sounds like a leftover from 1959,' frowns the man from the *NME* who sat on this year's

Ivor Novello panel and ought to know better when to certify originality. Over by Regent's Park, the thumb of *Music Now* isn't sure which way to swivel. 'Very dated (but effective) vocals, up tempo strings (but effective), freaky guitar (but effective) . . .'

Surely a hit?

'. . . No, I don't like it. Now tell me that Dib Cochran & The Earwigs are The Beatles in drag.'

The single is dismissed. The critics are wrong, but Marc and Tony aren't disheartened. Their next, they know, is not such an ugly duckling.

THE DOORBELL RINGS in Haddon Hall. David answers and sees Mike without his postbag but a large folder under his arm, smiling on his doorstep.

'It's finished,' he says.

David invites Mike inside. 'Mike's here,' he shouts to Angie.

Angie Busby-Berkeleys out of the bedroom like a one-woman *42nd Street*, surging into the living room where her eyes and David's lock cross hairs on Mike's hands as they open his folder and pull out a large piece of white card.

'So, this is it,' says Mike, smiling nervously.

It is a 12-inch square, hand-painted design in gouache dominated by one giant colour comic-book panel. On the right, a cowboy in a red jacket carries a wrapped rifle modelled on a publicity still of John Wayne in *The Searchers* from the 1957 *Picture Show* annual. The cowboy's Stetson disintegrates into the ether just like Mike's exploding-head Arts Lab posters, as David suggested. A speech bubble from his mouth. Mike had originally wanted the cowboy quoting a short story from J. G. Ballard's new collection, *The Atrocity Exhibition*, just published that summer.

But David didn't think the label would let them get away with it. Instead, Mike opts for harmless junkie double entendre.

Sleeves as in record sleeves, arms as in record arms.

Behind the cowboy, beneath a blanket of indigo twilight looms a foreboding grey mansion crowned by a distinctive clock tower. It is unmistakably The Cane. Mike copied it from a photo on a hospital leaflet. The title, *Metrobolist*, sits in the white border above in bold black Gothic lettering.

David glows. Angie sparkles.

Mike pulls out another piece of card with a separate illustration for the back cover. A peroxide-haired woman in a green party dress, arm in arm between two suitors, sharing another speech bubble.

The woman looks Monroeish but Mike's muse was Debbie Reynolds; he calls her Debbie Dagger. The suitor on her left in cap and overalls is based on the character of Jinkerman from Rex Warner's *The Professor*, an old orange Penguin paperback given to Mike by a Bromley communist and former lover of George Orwell. The suitor on her right is the legendary saint of Smokers' Corner, Ken Tapley.

'What do you think?' asks Mike.

'I LOVE IT!' Angie ticker-tapes and the matter is settled.

Angie explains that *Metrobolist* is going to have a gatefold sleeve. Mike's cowboy image will be the front, his 'Oh by jingo' trio somewhere on the back. The inner gatefold will be a collage of the photos of David in his Mr Fish dress.

'It's all going to work out,' promises Angie. 'It's all going to be fabulous.'

Mike is relieved Angie and David are so pleased. Maybe this is as good a time as any to ask for the return of his Andy Warhol Factory exhibition catalogue? But look at them, like a Medici duke and duchess marvelling over his handiwork. Glory be their *Metrobolist*. No, best not spoil the moment.

'Thanks,' says Mike.

Leave it until next time.

CONSTERNATION IN REGENT ARCADE HOUSE. Glossy colour prints of commercial suicide. Defries's Manhattan real estate, wearing a dress.

'Oh . . . *Christ!*'

Defries is appalled.

'Oh, David, David, *David.*'

So is Laurence. Not because one of his male artistes is wearing a dress which makes him look like a homosexual, but because one of his male artistes is wearing a dress which will make the general public *think* he is a homosexual. Goodbye pin-ups in *Jackie* and *Mirabelle*. Farewell Radio 1. Ta-ta *Top of the Pops*. Cheerio several thousand pounds of Laurence's money pissed down the drain of drag.

'What is he *thinking*?'

The Pre-Raphaelite Brotherhood. Dante Gabriel Rossetti and his many paintings of his married lover Jane Morris, wife of William, in particular her portrait as Shakespeare's Mariana from *Measure for Measure*. The same seated posture, leaning right, folds of silk, the same ripples of hair and bruised expression. *Blessed Damozel*.

That is what David is thinking: he just doesn't realise that in 1970 he's the only one who is.

EIGHTEEN

DOWN IN THE BIG CITY anything goes, but out in the suburbs the folks keep things just the way they like them. Especially ladies. The men here, they like a lady with legs, and they like that lady to show off them Betty Grables, all silky smooth, slidin' high to the top of the thigh. So they ain't too keen on this new limey fashion shit. The midi. Who wants a broad covering their gorgeous Grables in a long skirt? That's why all the menfolk, see, they got together with the local police chief. And then Mayor Baker, course he was all for it too. Then they held a council meeting and everyone agreed, so they went and made it a public law. Put up a sign and everything.

TO PROTECT THE INALIENABLE

RIGHT OF MAN TO ADMIRE

THE FEMALE FORM

MIDI-SKIRTS
ARE BANNED

IN THE COMMUNITY OF

HANOVER PARK, BY ORDER

You tell 'em! 'Most men around here are seriously against the midi.' Damn straight, Bill, this is America, 1970. 'I would certainly try, either by persuasion or ridicule, to prevent a girl wearing one.' And that's an attorney talking. 'We have asked the police department to look out for offenders and ask them to leave the streets.'

As for the women, why, they're all a-wigglin' their legs in their cute little ol' mini-skirts right beside 'em. We had stores round here that tried selling midis, but not any more. Bad trade. See, most women, they say the midi-skirt is all just a great big brainwashing operation. 'Why should we deprive our men of their pleasures? It's absolutely criminal.' Sure is, sister. Leave the crime and the deprivation to the Windy City folks. Hell, they ain't so far away as it is. Why it ain't 30 miles from Hanover Park down to The Loop and them big old skyscrapers on East Wacker Drive – hell knows what them folks do up *there* all day. You can bet they'll be looking at all kinds of depraved crap. Girls in midis? Jeezus, *guys* in midis! Shit, Mayor Baker, now he'd sure as hell have something to say about the inalienable rights of that one. *Goddamn!*

THE DOORBELL RINGS in Haddon Hall. David goes to answer it, blown on an American gust of screaming hellfire rushing behind him like water from a burst dam. Mike can see from David's face that something is wrong even before he's hit by the torrent. Trouble at *Metrobolist* mill.

'Come in,' says David.

'Is everything OK?'

'No. Mike . . . They've screwed up the sleeve.'

In the lounge, the dark green walls are aflame with Angie's ricochets of fury. Mike enters cautiously.

'HOW FUCKING *DARE* THEY! FUCKING *FASCISTS*!'

Seeing Mike, she slaps a palm to her forehead. 'Oh, Mike!' She puffs her cheeks. 'You will not *believe* what they've done!'

'Here.' David hands Mike a finished copy of the album that was *Metrobolist*. The first thing Mike notices is that it's no longer called *Metrobolist*. His lettering has been removed and in its place some lesser draughtsman has added their own comic-book script.

DAVID BOWIE
The Man Who $old The World

Mike is silent.

'See, they've changed the title,' says David.

'IT'S A *DISGRACE*!' seethes Angie. 'HOW FUCKING *DARE* THEY DICTATE HOW DAVID BE PRESENTED!'

The cowboy's words have also been blanked out. He still has a speech bubble but he's saying nothing.

'They've even fucked up the sound,' adds David.

Mike turns the album over. 'Oh by jingo.' Ken, Debbie and Jinkerman are still there at least. But there's no gatefold. No photos. No Pre-Raphaelite man in a midi-dress. No Mr Fish.

'They're *philistines*!' snaps Angie. 'Fucking *gangsters*! This would never have happened with Olav.'

Olav, once their Mercury/Philips man on the inside, is now their man on the outside, gone to RCA. David no longer has a Mercury/Philips man on the inside. All his guardian angels have flown the company coop. In their place are grey strangers in the offices of Stanhope Place fussing over The New Seekers and Blue Mink who vaguely recall a David Bowie.

Oh, you know? Odd little chap with curly hair . . . the one the Sketch *called a 'thin blond golliwog', remember? Did that space song with his funny little buzzing thing? Yes, that's him.*

They're the ones who sent off the artwork and master tapes to Mercury in Chicago where more grey strangers in a skyscraper down on East Wacker Drive – equally busy fussing over country by Bobby Bare and soul by Buddy Miles – no sooner slackened their jaws over Mike's gouache, 'Roll up your sleeves', the confusing title *Metrobolist* and all accompanying photos of a man in a midi-dress than they decided the American record-buying public must be spared such depravity at any cost.

Four thousand miles away, David remained oblivious to their art department's sabotage until a shipment of the finished record arrived at his front door. Only then did he fully understand his pitiful lack of creative control as it slid out of the box and into his hands where he gazed upon it with the same shock as if he'd just unboxed a severed head. There is nothing he can do. And when he asks, he's told there's nothing Defries can do either. This is it. *Metrobolist* is dead – long live *The Man Who $old The World*.

Mike is speechless. He scours the back sleeve again to see if he has a credit. He'd asked to be listed under the banner of 'Artists Union'. It isn't there.

'I don't know what to say,' says David.

'They've lobotomised it, haven't they?' says Mike.

The cowboy in his hands stares up, yelling dumbly.

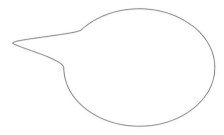

Nothing more need be said.

David lights a cigarette. Angie scowls at the ceiling, the scripts of tomorrow's terse phone calls boiling in her head like a tar barrel. A good time to make his excuses and leave, Mike decides.

'You can take that one,' says David.

He walks Mike with his LP to the front door.

'You'll still get paid for the cover,' he says. 'I'll make sure.'

On the doorstep, Mike remembers his Warhol catalogue. He'd really like it back. But the mood is bitter enough in there. No. Still not the right time.

'OK,' he says. 'See you, David.'

The door closes. A bite of winter in the air. Mike turns up his coat collar as he heads left onto Southend Road, his copy of *The Man Who $old The World* by David Bowie tucked tight under his arm. By the time he reaches Beckenham High Street he's smiling to himself – Hollywood visions of his art racked out in record shops all over the States. New York. San Francisco. Chicago. Los Angeles. Not the way he wanted it, but still, there he is. Ken Tapley over America.

Mike never sees his Warhol catalogue ever again.

★

'WHAT'S WRONG WITH YOUR TOWN?' *Rave* magazine wants to know but three hours north of Watford it's sorry it asked. A city centre with six cinemas, a theatre, an arts centre, a few discotheques, a swimming pool, a university, a bowling alley and a Mecca Locarno. A city where the kids aren't alright. The one Wimpy bar is a siege of coughing grown-ups. The arts centre hosts poetry readings for spec-polishing pseuds. The discotheques are strictly over-18. There's a municipal youth centre with one jukebox, stocked by adults. The rest is pubs upon pubs, working men's clubs, chippies and bingo. The wage rate here is way below the national average. Most kids can barely afford a bus into town from the tower-block gulags where there's nothing to do but loiter in packs marking time by the comings and goings of watchful police cars. Broken fences and smashed telephone boxes, trees planted in vain to prettify concrete death with natural life uprooted and abandoned as the plunders of boredom. This is no town to be of teen age.

'We want a disco,' a girl from the estates tells *Rave*, who pass her concerns to the council's youth vice-chairman. He is a retired teacher born in 1889. 'Young people used to enjoy all sorts of things,' he creaks. 'Physical education, woodwork, hockey. Now they don't want to do anything unless there's a noisy gramophone going. I've no objections to their having music if they did something else. But they've no other interests.'

His ear trumpet cannot accept that to be young in 1970 is to have no other interest than pop music. *Rave* retreats in defeat to write its obituary.

'Hull is that sort of city. A city where the quickest road out is the only bit that appeals to the young population.'

Verdict passed, the gallant reporting team take the quickest road to London and never look back. Somewhere far behind them, unheard in the vandalised gloom, a Les Paul pines.

NINETEEN

NEW BEGINNINGS. As the last leaves of summer brown, crinkle and fall so the dead skin of the Sixties flakes away with them. Jimi Hendrix marks Greta Garbo's 65th birthday by fatally choking on his own vomit in Notting Hill, three streets away from his poster hanging on the box room wall of 'Toadstool Studios'. Marc hears the news on his way to headlining a new festival near Glastonbury organised by a Somerset dairy farmer. A crowd of 1,500 pay the £1 ticket price to witness Jimi's ghost send shivers through Marc's fingers as a baton is passed from one electric warrior to another.

Death pays record company dividends and a two-year-old album track becomes Jimi's first number 1. 'Voodoo Chile' is not the closing of a coffin lid but the waking wail of a new age of pop paganism. The charts are spiritually possessed with black nights, Black Sabbath, shamanic Cherokee laments and frenzied Fräuleins hollering about witchcraft. Any colour of rock'n'roll, as long as it's black. 'We want to excite our audiences,' Brums Sabbath's fiddling gypsy Tony Iommi. 'But only with our music, which is mainly based on simple riffs and a heavy beat. Some people have put us down for this. But we like what we play and it seems that everyone else does. So that's it!'

Everyone likes Led Zeppelin's third album of Viking madrigals enough to rush it to number 1, though the group remain doggedly allergic to

142

the motion sickness of 45rpm. Instead, they consent to the surrogacy of producer Mickie Most's Collective Consciousness Society, or C.C.S., a studio band led by bluesman Alexis Korner who conducts an instrumental arrangement of the Zep's 'Whole Lotta Love'. Three weeks before it peaks at number 13, it's adopted as the new theme tune to a revamped *Top of the Pops*. The first episode also witnesses its own dance routine by Pan's People, who, this oestrogenic autumn of *The Female Eunuch*, the first Page 3 nipple and the flour-bombing of Bob Hope at Miss World, are finally allowed the minimum Equity wage. The Seventies find a cause and a revolution is televised.

New sounds demand new words and the word is *Sounds*.

'The new music of the Seventies deserves a paper of the Seventies. NOT a paper of the past desperately trying to keep up with it. *Sounds* is the weekly paper for the Seventies. The ONLY PAPER.'

The only paper for the Seventies lands in mourning black for Janis Joplin, gone the way of Jimi, featuring a survey on electric organs and the trials of Pink Floyd, who admit they may not be able to play their latest 13-minute indulgence, 'Alan's Psychedelic Breakfast', in concert since it would have to involve someone on stage frying eggs.

The message on the tablets: adapt or die.

Boots and braces are not working for a four-piece from Wolverhampton called Slade. The gamble they took one year ago to present themselves as a skinheads' rock band has failed. The stance says ska but the sound says Steppenwolf. The bigger problem is most bookers take one look at Slade and cry Strangeways. 'It began to affect promoters,' broods Noddy, their 24-year-old singer whose voice has been compared to Janis Joplin despite his being male and not yet dead on the cover of *Sounds*. 'They thought we were a bunch of idiots out to cause trouble.' Slade are neither idiots nor bovver boys. Hair and clothes can be changed, like luck. Their new album is called *Play It Loud*, and though nobody is listening yet, Slade are a long way from full volume.

But nothing is so loud as the sizzle of the Seventies' brightest new hope. He says his favourite colour is red, that he likes pets, art, soccer, tacos, Cokes and Elizabeth Montgomery from *Bewitched*. He doesn't like hotels and he doesn't like soup. He is 12-year-old Michael Jackson from Gary, Indiana, and he has two ambitions in life. Personally – 'to improve myself'. Professionally – 'to become a big star'. Bigger, no less beautiful ones are already aligning for him.

TODAY IT'S DAVID'S TURN to sever the past. A new song to be recorded in a new studio with a new producer and a newish band. The studio is in a deconsecrated church in Notting Hill roughly 500 yards from Marc's flat. The producer is Herbie Flowers, who David knows as the bass player from last year's 'Space Oddity' session. The musicians are those of Herbie's group, Blue Mink, who as moonlighting members of C.C.S. also play on the sexy new theme to *Top of the Pops*.

Herbie, real name Brian, is nearly ten years older than David. Flowers in more than name, he has horticultural medals for growing dahlias and tomatoes and also enjoys gliding, Katharine Hepburn movies, Constable paintings, Stravinsky and Sinatra. As a songwriter, Herbie's just made his mark as co-composer of Blue Mink's third hit, 'Our World', which is just about to fall out of the chart, as well as a new single by a popular sitcom actor which is just about to crash in.

A few months ago Herbie found himself at a celebrity gathering at Quaglino's restaurant in St James's thrown in honour of Ronnie Corbett who'd just been red-booked for an episode of *This Is Your Life* where surprise guest Danny La Rue skipped through the sliding doors wearing the exact same Mr Fish shirt and kipper tie as Corbett. How they howled. At the post-show celebrity dinner, Herbie – there through his connection with La Rue's Hanover Square club – was at the same table as another of Corbett's surprise guests, Clive Dunn from *Dad's Army*. When Clive found out Herbie was a musician and songwriter, he asked if he could compose something for the novelty album he was about to make for EMI based on his screen persona as senile fuzzy-wuzzy menace Corporal Jones. Together with his friend Kenny, former singer with art noise mods The Creation, Herbie came up with 'Grandad'. The words were a bit like one of David's old character songs from his first album when he used to sing about children, toffees and bombardiers. The tune was a clubfooted totter of brass and ivories, a bit like the theme from *Steptoe & Son*. Clive recorded it in a fatigued midnight session at Abbey Road after a day shooting *Dad's Army*. Herbie played the tuba.

This is the man who today is in charge of David's new direction.

The chosen song, intended as David's next single, is called 'Holy Holy', an intoxicated late offering to the prevailing pagan pop season. He sings about angels and devils and evil and righteousness, but its holiness is not wholly holy but unwholly about holding on to someone altogether unholy. Holy, as in David's shared lingering hippie obsession with deviant occultist Aleister Crowley, who apparently lived on a diet of 'eggs and heroin', one of the faces in the throng on *Sgt. Pepper*, subject of recent sexual magick pieces in *International Times*, and a whisper in the run-out grooves of the Zep's new album urging wanked-out teenage thieves of their sisters' Valderma to 'do what thou wilt'. Holy, as in his beloved Terry's beloved Ginsberg and his *Footnote to Howl*, with its world and soul and skin and nose and tongue and cock and hand and asshole and everything and everybody holy. Holy, as in Robin the Boy Wonder's holy blizzard, bat trap and barracuda. And more wholly holy as in David's wife. The sexual magick inside Haddon Hall has finally borne fruit. The son is to become a father. Angie, Madonna of the shocking pinks, is a holy mother-to-be.

David chooses to sing the song in a timbre that is not quite his own but more like how Marc used to sing a few years ago in a voice cross-legged and tasselly-cushioned. The voice fits the tune, which is also a bit cross-legged and tasselly-cushioned, if also a bit hay cart and earthenware jug. This must be what Herbie hears as he and his Blue Minkers Barry and Alan proceed to dismantle 'Holy Holy' one vibe at a time until all that remains is a partially electrified Morris dance. There is more sexual magick in 'Grandad' – and, for that matter, the theme to *Steptoe & Son*. Herbie's new direction for David is a clogged hop to oblivion, as anyone can hear.

Defries's ears are pure schmutter and hear nothing. He discusses whether the British version of the album that David still calls *Metrobolist* but which America knows as *The Man Who $old The World* should, when eventually released, also be called *Holy Holy* to capitalise on what he thinks will surely be David's next hit when it's released early in the new year. Defries employs an outside publicist who suggests the single be promoted as 'the first haunted song' – true only in the sense that it sounds like a seance vainly knocking for the lost spirit of Mick Ronson. Others at Gem hear all too clearly there isn't anybody there. 'Holy Holy' is breakfastly unplayable, Pan's Peopley undanceable and ungodly unsellable. The Seventies will be having none of it.

TWO DAYS LATER, while Led Zeppelin are breaking levees in the same Notting Hill studio vacated by David, one mile away in White City as Pan's People limber up to shiver their timber to 'Voodoo Chile', Marc prepares for his national pop coronation. 'Ride A White Swan' has charted. Last week, at 37. This week, up to 31. The papers dig it, from *Disc* to *Melody Maker*, who call it 'possibly the greatest advance in singles production since the Austrian Gustav von Pickup first demonstrated the possibilities of the triangular copper cylinder in 1937'. The DJs dig it too, from Blackburn at breakfast to Rosko at the weekend. Everyone digs it, apart from Alan Price who thinks 'it sounds like that Mungo Jerry fellow'. Price hasn't had a Top 10 hit in three years, and the fact that he considers 'Ride A White Swan' 'monotonous' explains why: in T. Rex he hears the firing squad of his own obsolescence. Today Marc loads the gun. Tomorrow the trigger pulls at five past seven on BBC 1. Marc is *Top of the Pops*.

Only a few weeks ago he told Her Royal Hi-fi-ness Penny Valentine he didn't think T. Rex would be allowed on *Top of the Pops*. 'I'm sure the people there think we're weirdos.' Perhaps forgetting there is no bigger weirdo at *Top of the Pops* than Jimmy Savile.

'It's useful to be Jimmy Savile,' brags Jim, 'and have a bit of power if you can make it work for you and others. You can even screw some people sometimes.' This week Jim is trying to screw the *NME*. A few episodes ago he asked a black girl in the studio audience where she was from. 'Hammersmith,' said the girl. 'Could've fooled me,' jimmied Jim. The *NME* dared to suggest he was being racist. A morally outraged Jim demanded an apology. 'Remarks of mine like "could've fooled me" have been going on for years and don't mean a thing. To invest them, all of a sudden, with dire racialist meaning is quite unbelievable!' Quite unbelievably, Jim tells another pop paper how he recently swindled a hi-fi shop into selling him a stereo for half its value because he needed it for a disco at Broadmoor Hospital for the Criminally Insane. 'Because he's Jimmy Savile he gets away with murder,' laughs the man from *Disc*. History pretends not to hear, nor to see those hiding in its plainest sight.

Luckily for Marc, his *Top of the Pops* debut falls on a rotating week hosted by Blackburn. The other studio acts include The Move, the Bee Gees and Dave Edmunds, whose 'I Hear You Knocking' will soon freeze at the top of the charts until the first thaw of January. Edmunds' tune is a bump back to the rocking Fifties. T. Rex's bumps the Fifties into the shocking present. For most people watching, this is their first glimpse of Marc: a curly cherubic tease, topless under blue velvet dungarees twirling a Les Paul stripped to the wood, which, just like Mick's, glistens gold under the lights. It's also their first salivating glimpse of Mickey, seated on Marc's right pretending to play the bass, which he can't – not that anyone hot-flushing at home is transfixed by his fret hand. The sight and sound of T. Rex is like discovering a new dial on the TV set that allows the viewer to see and hear things never seen or heard before. A crystal ball into another Eden.

It's the kids who see furthest and hear loudest. As Marc well knows, the kids are the ones who hold all the power in rock'n'roll. They always have done. He'd held it himself when he was a 9-year-old trembling on his bedroom floor to the angel of the Lord singing 'Blue Suede Shoes', his life decided before the liquor hit the bottom of the old fruit jar. Rock'n'roll was the circus of his runaway dreams. Heeding two for the show, he ran away and joined it. But without the kids there isn't any circus. Marc, now the rock'n'roll ringmaster of T. Rex, needs those kids. The ones marooned in Thamesmead, Bransholme, Toxteth, Castlemilk, Splott and the sticks of Fuckallshire whose material devotion to pop music is forever at the mercy of pocket money and the distance to the nearest Woolworths. The ones with big dreams but no bread. So Marc's going to save them.

His masterplan is to make T. Rex not just the greatest rock'n'roll band the kids have ever heard but the most affordable. He'll give them the stars and charge them a pebble. The kids are too skint to buy albums, so, starting with 'Ride A White Swan', he'll make every T. Rex single a three-tracker with *two* B-sides so they get maximum thrilling for their shilling. The kids are too skint to go to concerts so he arranges a tour at bargain ticket prices. 'It's more help for the kids if we can do it cheaper,' says Marc. 'T. REX PLAY WOODLAND ROCK FOR THE CHILDREN OF THE UNIVERSE,' says the ad.

T. Rex *is* our universe, say the kids.

Top of the Pops catapults 'Ride A White Swan' into the Top 20, earning them a second Savile-free visit. Marc likens it to being in a Fellini film. Soon enough he finds his dolce vita: the following week T. Rex are in the Top 10.

'I have always wanted a hit record more than anything,' confesses Marc. 'I was very near to giving up. But the gods have been very kind. Everything has fallen into place beautifully.'

Blessed by the gods, Marc falls into place beside Steve McQueen, Paul Newman, Robert Redford and Elvis in *Honey* magazine's calendar hunks for 1971. Giddy with triumph, he tells the kids 'Swan' is the first battle won in a holy pop war. The papers ask him to name the enemy. 'Songwriters like Tony Macaulay.' T. Rex are the cavalry come to tear down all Edison Lighthouses and their keepers.

'T. Rex really were a little silly saying that,' tuts Macaulay. 'We manage them. Or at least my company does. I've never had to stoop to copying Mungo Jerry for ideas, and never resorted to two chords and thin microscopic vocals. All they produce is synthetic pop that's trying to be encompassed under an underground roof.'

Macaulay has sweet reason to be bitter. It was his ex-girlfriend, Anya, who championed T. Rex into the charts in her capacity as an independent radio plugger. It also doesn't help that Macaulay's latest, 'Blame It On The Pony Express', almost flung to Edison Lighthouse but tossed instead to Johnny Johnson & His Bandwagon, is this week lagging three places behind 'Ride A White Swan'. And he's wrong about them sharing management. Macaulay's company is Gem: possibly he's muddling Marc with their other oddball, David Bowie.

Gloves off, Marc delivers the final slap in an open letter which makes front-page pop news.

'I would like to enlighten Tony Macaulay on two matters which seem to be giving some confusion. Firstly, neither T. Rex nor our managers are connected in any way with Mr Macaulay or his company. Secondly, I don't really think that anybody with any musical awareness of the last three years could seriously accuse us of

copying Mungo Jerry. It's obvious from Tony Macaulay's comments that he knows little about T. Rex or our music – but don't Blame It On The Pony Express.
   Love Grows,
   Marc Bolan.'

BASHED, DEMONISED, MOCKED and harassed. The brothers and sisters have had enough. Another of their own, Louis the Young Liberal, caught bang to rights cruising in a park in Islington. The pigs say 'importuning'. The brothers and sisters say 'police entrapment'. Louis doesn't want the attention but the brothers and sisters want liberation and in his name they demand it.

Friday-night curtains twitch to spy 150 of them marching by torchlight around Highbury Fields. Brothers hand in hand with brothers, sisters kissing sisters, holding balloons and candles chanting 'GIVE US A G!' and 'RIGHT ON!' A scribble of reporters watch and listen to the frightening demands of these permissives on parade. To cease the discrimination against gay people on the streets and in the workplace. To end exclusive heterosexual sex education in schools and the treatment of homosexuality as a psychiatric illness. To reduce the age of consent for gay males to the same age as straight males. And to ensure all people attracted to a member of their own sex be taught that such feelings are perfectly normal.

'GAY POWER TO GAY PEOPLE! ALL POWER TO OPPRESSED PEOPLE!'

The first mass demonstration of gay pride on British soil ends without arrest in the victory haze of last orders at The Cock. Until the Saturday hangover brings the defeated realisation that none of the reporters' shorthand has made newsprint. Not for the mockery of the redtops. Not for the moral disgust of the *Mail*. Not for the solidarity of the *Morning Star*. Not for the elbow-patched empathy of the *Guardian*. Not even for the local gossip of that week's *Islington Gazette*. The existence of a Gay Liberation Front shall not yet speak its name in a land where big news means photographic evidence of Monika Dietrich's 38-inch bust.

The Front are disappointed but not remotely surprised, and within a week respond with the launch of their own pamphlet. 'All those so-called gay mags such as *Jeremy* are just a load of absolute bullshit,' hisses issue one of *Come Together*, unaware that poor *Jeremy* folded back in the summer after only nine issues. 'From now on, gay people in Britain are going to write *their own* history.'

The closet queendom dead, the brothers and sisters hail the new republic. Leading those brave enough to follow beyond themselves, where there is grace and beauty, gaiety and freedom . . .

'**WILL THEY NOT FOLLOW US?** *We'll lead them beyond themselves, where there is grace and beauty, gaiety and freedom.'*

Sensual, electric Garbo heads the charge. Prime-time BBC 1, the channel that brought you *Steptoe* 'poofmania' now bringing you the bed-hopping tragedy of a bisexual monarch in 17th-century Sweden. She kisses a countess full on the lips and flirts with a busty parlourmaid. She dresses as a man and is mistaken as such by a rakish Spanish envoy who falls in love with *him* before he falls in love with *her*. As two 'men' they share a bed at a country inn where a confused valet thinks they must be a couple of homosexuals. 'Forgive me for being a queen,' melts Garbo. And it's still only quarter past nine.

In 1933 Garbo is *Queen Christina*. In 1970 she is Queen of England when the BBC show five of her films for the first time on British TV under the series banner *Garbo the Incomparable*. The nation's press are just as lost for adjectives. The art critics in the Sunday broadsheets. The stylists in *19*. Jean Rook in the *Sketch*. Even the hippies in *Friends*. Any excuse to write about her radioactive beauty and intoxicating melancholy, the Englishman she never met who left her £5,000 in his will, the Frenchman who ran towards the cinema screen to kiss her face, the time Richard Burton asked if he could kiss her knee, the vont-to-be-aloneness of the greatest star that ever lived, now a 65-year-old Manhattan recluse of paparazzi big game.

Outside in the cold, the Seventies' first December is a bleak winterland of sleet, ice, power cuts and blackouts.

'*The snow is like a wide sea. One could go out and get lost in it. Forget the world and oneself.'*

Garbo's eyes smoulder on David's mantelpiece as they do on the screen. This is his second winter in Haddon Hall but the first Christmas he and Angie will spend together: the two of them, soon to be three of them. At 14 weeks, Angie's not showing, just planning. Angie is never not planning. New colours. Greens to pinks, silvers to golds. Different rooms. Move a bed here, a dining table there. Visions. Ideas. Changes.

'I'm not an idle woman . . . I have a war on my hands.'

They may have to ask David's mother over this Christmas. The two Mrs Joneses have to suffer one another a lot more since they found Peggy her own flat within walking distance down on Albemarle Road. She'll also want to visit the hospital at some point. There's lots that goes on up The Cane at Christmas, says Peggy. Carols, film shows, musical chairs, balloon races. Even fancy dress.

'The wind is with us.'

Ten to ten, the gales blow but a nation is spellbound by the eyes of infinity. Queen Christina has given up her throne to sail away with the one she loves but when she reaches the ship she finds him wounded and dying. He passes away in her arms. Her love boat becomes a funeral cortège accompanying his body back to his homeland having sacrificed her own forever. Garbo takes position on the prow like the figurehead of a Norse ocean goddess, staring out across the sea further than all imaginable time. Stoic eyes like thin sheets of ice over two bottomless wells of loneliness.

Just like the look in David's eyes when he hears Marc's now a pop star and it hits him, like a lover dying in his arms, that one year since *he* was, he no longer is.

Extreme close-up. Orchestra crescendo. Fade to black.

THE END

Or perhaps just the beginning. There is a Les Paul in Hull and its white knight to rescue. There are verses to be written and cheeks to be powdered. There are battles to fight and lives to save. There are things to be and shapes to come. There is history to make and a world to win. There is a future to remember and a past to forget. There are ghosts. There are regrets. But there are still stars to wish upon.

BOWIEDISCOGRAPHY70

March   **'The Prettiest Star'**
b/w 'Conversation Piece'
Mercury MF1135 (mono). A-side replaced original single choice of 'London Bye Ta-Ta'. *B-side recorded in 1969 during sessions for the album* David Bowie.

The World Of David Bowie
'Uncle Arthur', 'Love You Till Tuesday', 'There Is A Happy Land', 'Little Bombardier', 'Sell Me A Coat', 'Silly Boy Blue', 'The London Boys' / 'Karma Man', 'Rubber Band', 'Let Me Sleep Beside You', 'Come And Buy My Toys', 'She's Got Medals', 'In The Heat Of The Morning', 'When I Live My Dream'
Decca PA58 (mono) SPA58 (stereo). Compilation album of material recorded under contract to the Deram label 1966–68.

June   **'Memory Of A Free Festival (Part 1)'**
b/w 'Memory Of A Free Festival (Part 2)'
Mercury 6052 026.

BOWIESOURCES70

AUTHOR INTERVIEWS in person, by telephone and additional email correspondence with Angie Bowie Barnett, John Cambridge, Gerald Chevin, Nita Clarke, Laurence Myers, Tony Visconti, Michael J. Weller and Anya Wilson. For eleventh-hour assistance thanks also to Mark Pritchett.

The memoirs of Angie Bowie, *Free Spirit* (Mushroom Books, 1981) and *Backstage Passes: Life on the Wild Side with David Bowie* (with Patrick Carr, Putnam, 1993); Laurence Myers, *Hunky Dory (Who Knew?)* (B&B Books, 2019); Kenneth Pitt, *Bowie: The Pitt Report* (Omnibus Press, 1985); Tony Visconti, *Bowie, Bolan and the Brooklyn Boy* (HarperCollins, 2007); Woody Woodmansey, *Spider from Mars: My Life with Bowie* (Sidgwick & Jackson, 2016).

Kevin Cann's indispensable *Any Day Now: David Bowie: The London Years 1947–74* (Adelita, 2010), the road map on which all Bowie biographers travel.

Other works: Victoria Broackes & Geoffrey Marsh, *David Bowie Is* (V&A Publications, 2013); David Buckley, *Strange Fascination: Bowie: The Definitive Story* (Virgin, 2000); Kevin Cann, *David Bowie: A Chronology* (Vermilion, 1983); Neil Cossar, *David Bowie: I Was There* (Red Planet, 2017); Mary Finnigan, *Psychedelic Suburbia: David Bowie and the Beckenham Arts Lab* (Jorvik Press, 2016); Peter & Leni Gillman, *Alias David Bowie* (New English Library, 1987); Roger Griffin, *David Bowie: The Golden Years*

(Omnibus Press, 2016); Jerry Hopkins, *Bowie* (Elm Tree, 1985); Dylan Jones, *David Bowie: A Life* (Windmill Books, 2018); Lesley-Ann Jones, *Hero: David Bowie* (Hodder & Stoughton, 2016), and *Ride a White Swan: The Lives and Death of Marc Bolan* (Hodder & Stoughton, 2012); Wendy Leigh, *Bowie: The Biography* (Gallery Books, 2016); Cliff McLenehan, *Marc Bolan: 1947–1977 A Chronology* (Helter Skelter, 2002); Paul Morley, *The Age of Bowie* (Simon & Schuster, 2016); John O'Connell, *Bowie's Books: The Hundred Literary Heroes Who Changed His Life* (Bloomsbury, 2019); Chris O'Leary, *Rebel Rebel: All the Songs of David Bowie from '64 to '76* (Zero Books, 2015); Mark Paytress, *Bolan: The Rise and Fall of a 20th Century Superstar* (Omnibus Press, 2006); Norman J. Sheffield, *Life on Two Legs: Set the Record Straight* (Trident Publishing, 2013); George Tremlett, *The David Bowie Story* (Futura, 1974); Paul Trynka, *Starman: David Bowie: The Definitive Biography* (Sphere, 2011); Aubrey Walter (ed.), *Come Together: The Years of Gay Liberation 1970–73* (Gay Men's Press, 1980); Weird & Gilly, *Mick Ronson: The Spider with the Platinum Hair* (Independent Music Press, 2009); Michael J. Weller, *Metrobolist: Five Chapters*, a series of chapbooks (Home Baked Books, 2015).

Information on Cane Hill Hospital courtesy of testimonies, Pam Buttrey's *Cane Hill Hospital: The Tower on the Hill* (Aubrey Warbash Publishing, 2010) and the kind assistance of Lindsay Ould at the Museum of Croydon. Other than Terry Burns, the names of other Cane Hill cases have been changed. Also referenced were R. D. Laing's works *The Divided Self: An Existential Study in Sanity and Madness* (1960), *Sanity, Madness and the Family* (with Aaron Esterson, 1964) and *The Politics of Experience and the Bird of Paradise* (1967), all published by Pelican/Penguin.

Key period broadcasts referenced: *Doomwatch*, 'Survival Code' (BBC, 1970), written by Kit Pedler and Gerry Davis; *Queen Christina* (MGM, 1933), written by S. N. Behrman and Ben Hecht, screenplay by H. M. Harwood and Salka Viertel; *Steptoe & Son*, 'Any Old Iron' (BBC, 1970), written by Ray Galton and Alan Simpson.

Period newspapers and magazines. National: *Daily Express, Daily Mail, Daily Mirror, Daily Sketch, The Guardian, News of the World, Radio Times, The Sun, The Sunday Times* (and *Magazine*), *The Times, TV Times.*

Regional: *Beckenham Journal, Bromley & Kentish Evening Times, Evening Standard* (London), *Hull & Yorkshire Times, Press & Journal* (Aberdeen).

Pop/teenage: *Disc & Music Echo, Fabulous 208, Honey, Jackie, Melody Maker, Mirabelle, Music Now, New Musical Express, 19, Rave, Record Mirror, Sounds* (launched October 1970); with very special thanks to the archives of Tom Sheehan.

Counterculture and gay: *Come Together, Friends, International Times, Jeremy* (nine issues, September 1969 to May 1970), *Time Out* (the London listings magazine, in 1970 still associated with the underground press).

For additional liaising, clarifying and lead suggesting thanks to Ali Costelloe, Peter Myers and Neil Parkinson at the Royal College of Art.

BOWIEIMAGES70

IMAGES pages 6–7

Top row (left to right): Robert Powell as English martyr Toby Wren (© BBC Photo Sales); Anthony Newley, in his solitude (© Studio Canal/ Shutterstock); Coming to the boil in Haddon Hall's converted cloakroom kitchen, 1970 (© Pictorial Press Ltd/Alamy).

Bottom row (left to right): T. Rex's too sexy Marc Bolan and Mickey Finn (© Gijsbert Hanekroot/Redferns/Getty); The fleshpots of St Anne's Court, Soho, some 50 yards along from Trident studios near the Dean Street exit, February 1970 (© Aubrey Hart/Evening News/Shutterstock); The birth of grunge (© Pictorial Press Ltd/Alamy).

IMAGES page 8

David gazes a gazeless stare, the garden of Haddon Hall, Beckenham, autumn 1970 (© Pictorial Press Ltd/Alamy).

ENDPAPERS

Antiques floorshow – David reclines in Haddon Hall, 1970 (© Pictorial Press Ltd/Alamy).

Picture research and layout concept by Simon Goddard.

THANKYOU

Angie Bowie Barnett for her thoughts, conversation
and thoughts on our conversation.

John Cambridge, the pivotal Hull's angel in Bowie's story
and the kindest of northern souls.

Michael J. Weller for opening the gate to his wonderful
Wellerverse and the fruits of its allotment.

To the city of Hull, with love from one who lived there. Neither I nor
Bowie would have done what we did without you.

David Barraclough at Omnibus for the original idea, and Kevin
Pocklington at The North Literary Agency for making it happen.

The Three Graces – Alison Rae for her Raegun to the head,
Imogen Gordon Clark and Debra Geddes at Great Northern PR.

And to Sylv, and to our friends for being there.

DAVID BOWIE
will return in

BOWIEODYSSEY**71**

COMING 2021